Bermuda

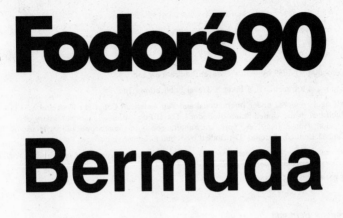

Fodor's 90
Bermuda

FODOR'S TRAVEL PUBLICATIONS, INC.
New York & London

Fodor's Bermuda

Editors: Jacqui Russell, Kathy Ewald
Area Editor: Sandra Hart
Drawings: Ted Burwell
Photographs: Bermuda Department of Tourism
Maps: Clarice Borio
Cover Photograph: Paul Barton

Cover Design: Vignelli Associates

Special Sales

Fodor's Travel Publications are available at special discounts for bulk purchases (100
copies or more) for sales promotions or premiums. Special editions, including personalized
covers, excerpts of existing guides, and corporate imprints, can be created in large
quantities for special needs. For more information, write to Special Marketing, Fodor's
Travel Publications, 201 East 50th Street, New York, NY 10022. Enquiries from the
United Kingdom should be sent to Fodor's Travel Publications, 30–32 Bedford Square,
London WC1B 3SG.

CONTENTS

v

CONTENTS

FOREWORD

While every care has been taken to assure the accuracy of the information in this guide, the passage of time will always bring change, and consequently, the publisher cannot accept responsibility for errors that may occur.

All prices and opening times quoted here are based on information available to us at press time. Hours and admission fees may change, however, and the prudent traveler will avoid inconvenience by calling ahead.

Fodor's wants to hear about your travel experiences, both pleasant and unpleasant. When a hotel or restaurant fails to live up to its billing, let us know and we will investigate the complaint and revise our entries where the facts warrant it.

Send your letters to the editors of Fodor's Travel Publications, 201 E. 50th Street, New York, NY 10022.

FACTS AT YOUR FINGERTIPS

FACTS AT YOUR FINGERTIPS

Planning Your Trip

WHAT WILL IT COST? Bermuda is a quality resort island—there is no doubt. Although it is one of the smallest countries in the world, it ranks sixth among the world's richest. According to World Bank figures, the island's average annual household income is over $20,000, ranking only behind the United Arab Emirates, Kuwait, Qatar, Switzerland, and Sweden. All this makes for a most expensive atmosphere to the visitor! In fact, the Bermuda Department of Tourism concentrates on appealing to households earning greater than $50,000 per year with additional emphasis on a younger group of visitors (honeymooners, college students) who represent the potential of repeat business.

Expect high prices everywhere in Bermuda (accommodations, food, drink, motorcycle rentals, etc.) and gear your budget accordingly. There really are accommodations to fit almost every pocketbook, from the $150 per-person, per-day variety down to less than $35. If your heart is set on Bermuda, do your own homework and gather free information from the Bermuda Departments of Tourism in New York, Boston, Atlanta, Chicago, and Toronto. Talk very seriously to a knowledgeable travel agent who has been to the island very recently and can personally recommend several categories of accommodations.

There are excellent package trips to Bermuda, some of them much less expensive than others. These feature the famous honeymooners programs, as well as those for golfers, tennis nuts, and families. Prices are highest from April to mid-November, then drop considerably during the cooler and less-crowded winter months. May, June, September, and all long holiday weekends are popular, so book well ahead. Airfares are still reasonable from anywhere in North America. One-week cruises from New York offer the best of both worlds.

Food, drink, and taxis are expensive, but the island's natural beauty is free. You can rent motorbikes by the week and save, or take local buses and ferries. Most of the local beaches are public, and tennis-court rentals and greens fees tend to be reasonable.

You will also save money if you stay in a housekeeping cottage (large) for about $50 per day or in a smaller unit for approximately $40 per day. While food is expensive in the local supermarkets, it is even more costly in restaurants. Guest houses are especially economical, and some offer bed and breakfast for about $35 per day (but no cooking for dinner). See your travel agent for more economical advice.

WHEN TO GO. Anytime! Bermuda is a year-round resort with a mild, subtropical climate. Winters may be cool and windy, but they are perfect for golf and tennis. The Department of Tourism has daily events planned for visitors during the winter. Spring comes early, and with it the college crowd arrives for five weeks of fun and frolic. June and September are tra-

Monthly Average Daily Temperature

Month	Air				Sea		Relative Humidity
	Max.		Min.				
	C.	F.	C.	F.	C.	F.	%
Jan.	20.8	(69.4)	15.7	(60.2)	16.7	(62)	77
Feb.	20.0	(68.0)	14.9	(58.9)	16.1	(61)	74
Mar.	20.3	(68.5)	15.3	(59.6)	17.8	(64)	72
Apr.	21.3	(70.4)	15.7	(60.3)	18.3	(65)	74
May	23.5	(74.3)	18.7	(65.6)	22.8	(73)	81
Jun.	26.5	(79.7)	21.4	(70.5)	25.0	(77)	79
Jul.	28.4	(83.1)	23.3	(74.0)	26.7	(80)	77
Aug.	29.4	(85.0)	23.8	(74.9)	28.9	(84)	77
Sep.	28.9	(84.1)	22.7	(72.9)	26.7	(80)	75
Oct.	26.2	(79.2)	21.3	(70.3)	25.0	(77)	75
Nov.	23.3	(73.9)	17.9	(64.3)	21.1	(70)	70
Dec.	21.1	(70.0)	15.9	(60.7)	18.3	(65)	72

The nighttime temperature is approximately 5°C(19°F) cooler than the daily high temperature.

Sunshine and Rainfall

Month	Daily Average Hours of Sunshine	Monthly Average Rainfall	
		mm	inches
January	5.1	103.12	4.06
February	5.4	128.27	5.05
March	6.3	117.60	4.63
April	7.5	76.45	3.01
May	8.2	98.04	3.86
June	8.6	131.32	5.17
July	9.9	101.09	3.98
August	9.0	133.86	5.27
September	7.9	133.35	5.25
October	6.3	152.91	6.02
November	5.8	133.79	4.48
December	4.9	97.03	3.82

ditional months for honeymooners. The official beach season opens the 24th of May and goes through September. Most of the hotels and larger cottage colonies have heated pools.

The island's summer temperatures are in the 70s and 80s (F.), and the days are generally warm and sunny through November. There has never been a year with less than 340 days of recorded sunshine and the average is 351 days. The lowest temperature officially recorded is 41 degrees F. in 1955 and annual rainfall is approximately 57 inches, spread evenly throughout the 12 months. Rainfall is usually of brief duration and the skies normally clear very quickly.

HOW TO GO. The Bermuda Department of Tourism publishes a number of attractive brochures on Bermuda and stays in close contact with travel agents, keeping them abreast of the latest developments in facilities, rates, and booking trends. Therefore, the department suggests that you discuss your holiday plans with a travel agent who knows Bermuda. If you do not have a travel agent, the **American Society of Travel Agents,** 1101 King Street, Alexandria, VA 22314; the **Association of Canadian Travel Agents,** 130 Albert Street, Suite 1207, Ottawa, Ontario; or the **Association of British Travel Agents,** 55 Newman Street, London W1P 4AH, will advise you.

HOW TO GET THERE. Most airlines publish brochures on Bermuda and offer special tours and packages, ranging from honeymoon to sports programs. *American Airlines* flies daily direct from New York's La-Guardia and Boston.

Delta Airlines flies daily from Atlanta, Boston, and Hartford with the same fares available, with a number of excellent honeymoon, golf, and tennis packages.

Pan Am has daily flights from JFK Airport in New York. Pan Am pioneered air service to Bermuda with the famous Martin 130 "flying boat," which landed off Darrell's Island.

Air Canada offers nonstop service from Toronto (four times weekly in summer, five times weekly in winter) with connecting services from all of Canada as well as connections with the New York/Bermuda carriers.

British Airways flies daily from London, the Caribbean, South America, and Tampa. British Airways offers special one- and two-week holidays in Bermuda.

A few years ago, the Bermuda government relaxed its policy on charter flights and now permits public charters to call at the island. The charters are permitted from nongateway cities and from designated gateway cities not served by nonstop scheduled service. The new rules allow many more visitors from North America to enjoy Bermuda.

By Sea: The glamorous days of cruising to Bermuda and back are not over! Between April first and late November, one can board a luxury cruise vessel in New York and sail to Bermuda on a choice of ships. Other ships call at the island from Norfolk, Port Everglades, Miami, and European ports. A one-week cruise to Bermuda combines the best of both worlds. On board, there is plenty of time to relax and rest, be pampered by an attentive crew, meet the captain at his complimentary cocktail party, and become acquainted with fellow passengers. One has only to choose the lifestyle one prefers at sea.

The 710-passenger *Bermuda Star* divides her time between the ports of St. George's and Hamilton, offering a taste of both capitals. The shipline is treating the *Bermuda Star* as a first-class New York hotel, with piano bar, a string quartet in the dining room, and specialties prepared at your table by the maitre d'. The Saturday afternoon departures from New York return the following Saturday about 8 A.M.

Royal Caribbean Cruise Line's *Nordic Prince* continues mid-weekly New York to Bermuda sailings from mid-April through September. The 23,200-ton *Nordic Prince* has a passenger capacity of 1,038. The Line's other ships are the *Song of Norway* and the *Sun Viking*. Chandris Fantasy Cruises' *Galileo* and *Amerikanis* offer 6-night cruises originating in New York from May to October.

When Home Lines ceased operation last year, the Cunard Line returned with its *Cunard Princess,* for one-week cruises from New York May 17 to October 11. The *Princess* leaves New York on Wednesday, docks at St. George's on Friday and at Hamilton on Saturday and Sunday, making her the only ship in port on the weekend. Cunard offers either the round-trip cruise, or a one-way sail to Bermuda with the return by air.

Royal Viking's *Star* also makes week-long cruises from New York the end of April through mid-October. She leaves New York on Saturday, arrives in Hamilton on Monday, leaves Bermuda on Thursday, and returns to New York early Saturday morning.

One-week cruises to Bermuda from New York range from approximately $150 to $350 per person, per day (double occupancy), depending upon what category of accommodation you prefer. The price includes all meals and facilities of the ship.

TOURIST INFORMATION. The *Bermuda Department of Tourism* is located in the U.S. at: 310 Madison Ave., New York, N.Y. 10017; Suite 1010, 44 School St., Boston, Mass. 02108; 235 Peachtree St., N.E., Atlanta, Ga. 30303; 150 N. Wacker Drive, Chicago, Ill. 60606. On the west coast: John A. Tetley, Inc., 3075 Wilshire Blvd., Los Angeles, CA 90010. In Canada: 1200 Bay Street, Toronto M5R 2A5. In the U.K.: BCB Ltd., 6 Burnsall St., London SW3 3ST.

In Bermuda, the department is located in Global House, 43 Church St., Hamilton. *Visitors Service Bureau* is located at the Ferry Dock in Hamilton, Bermuda Airport, King's Square in St. George's, and in the lovely village of Somerset. The *Bermuda Hotel Association* is on the corner of King and Reid streets in Hamilton.

The Department of Tourism publishes free of charge "Bermuda," "Bermuda Travel Tips," "Handy Reference Map," "Sportsman's Guide to Bermuda," and many other helpful brochures. In addition, "This Week in Bermuda" and "Preview of Bermuda" are available for free in shops, hotels, and tourist facilities. Cruise passengers will find on board their vessels free brochures about Bermuda.

There are excellent bookstores in Bermuda and literature on local history, legend, flora, etc., is abundant. Local historians include William Zuill (director of the Bermuda National Trust) and the late Terry Tucker, the island's most prolific writer.

WHAT TO TAKE. The prerequisite for any holiday trip is to pack clothes that are comfortable and climate-ready. In Bermuda, daytime life is informal but dignified. Dress pants or designer jeans for women are acceptable, but short shorts and bare feet are not appreciated. Evening wear is more formal, especially if you are staying in a hotel or cottage colony. Jacket and tie are required in upscale dining rooms.

During the warmer months, May through November, lightweight cotton or drip-dry fabrics are most suitable. Men will need a lightweight jacket in the evening and women should bring a shawl or fancy sweater. Bathing suits, tennis and golf clothes, and a lightweight raincoat should also be packed. This is real Bermuda shorts season, especially if you plan to travel around by motorbike (bathing suits, bare feet, or being shirtless are not permitted on cycles).

During the colder months, from mid-November through April, bring some warm woolens and a heavy jacket. During the day, wool skirts, slacks, and sweaters are necessary. The nights are even cooler. But Bermuda weather is variable on any given day and the visitor must be prepared to peel or add layers as necessary. Sudden squalls make it necessary to carry a handy, portable umbrella or light raincoat at all times. You'll want to bring bathing suits (for indoor or heated pools), and golf and tennis clothes even in the cooler months.

Should you forget an item, or wish you had another outfit to wear, there are tempting buys in clothes for both men and women. Sweaters, skirts, slacks, and jackets from Britain, as well as resort-type clothes from around the world, fill the shops on Front Street and their branches throughout the island. Imported goods are expensive, however, so shop carefully.

Golf, tennis, scuba diving, and snorkeling equipment is available for rental throughout the island, but riding enthusiasts should bring their own gear. All kinds of camera equipment can be bought in Bermuda. Many hotels, gift shops, and photo dealers offer one-day service on Kodacolor, Ektachrome, and black and white film. As the sun is very bright, check suggested settings with a photo dealer or use a light meter.

TRAVEL DOCUMENTS. Passports and visas are not required except for Iron-Curtain nationals, Cubans, Argentinians, Nicaraguans, Iranians, Libyans, etc. At the time of entry into Bermuda, a return or outward-bound ticket as well as proof of citizenship of the U.S. or Canada is required for those citizens. This proof may be a valid passport, birth certificate, U.S. Naturalization Certificate, or / U.S. Alien Registration card. All bona fide visitors to the colony may remain for a period of three weeks from arrival date. After this period, they must apply for an extended stay to the Chief Immigration Officer. **Note:** Visitors are not allowed to conduct any business in Bermuda without a special permit and this law is strictly enforced. Contact the Chamber of Commerce (Ferry Dock, Hamilton) for information.

CUSTOMS REGULATIONS. Visitors may bring into the colony, duty-free, all personal clothing, cameras, sports equipment, etc. They may also bring 50 cigars, 200 cigarettes, one pound of tobacco, one quart of liquor, and one quart of wine. Importing illegal drugs (including marijuana) is an offense and subject to fines of up to $5,000 or three years imprisonment, or both. Visitors are requested to declare all prescription drugs.

PETS. Permits must be obtained well in advance from the Director, Department of Agriculture, Box HM 834, Hamilton HM CX, Bermuda, for the importation of all animals (including household pets) into Bermuda. Airlines are allowed to carry the pets, either as excess baggage or cargo, but cruise ships are *not.* Dogs and other pets are permitted at some hotels and guest houses, but permission must be obtained in advance and, generally, only small, well-trained pets are allowed.

MONEY. The Bermuda dollar (BD$) has been linked to the U.S. dollar since August 1977 and is accepted at par in shops, restaurants, and hotels. Canadian currency is also accepted but may be discounted. The British pound and all other currencies must be exchanged at Bermuda banks for local tender. U.S. travelers' checks are accepted everywhere. Credit cards may be used to pay most hotel bills and are accepted in many shops and restaurants.

On the reverse side of all Bermuda notes is a portrait of Queen Elizabeth II. The blue $1 note pictures Bermuda-fitted dinghies racing. The maroon $5 note features St. David's Lighthouse; the mauve $10 note shows the longtail bird. The green $20 note has Somerset Bridge, and the brown $50 note features Gibbs Hill Lighthouse. The same picture of the queen that is found on British coinage is also on the reverse side of all Bermuda coins. The 50-cent piece has Bermuda's coat of arms; the 25-cent piece, the longtail bird; the 10-cent piece, Bermuda lilies; the $1 coin and the 5-cent piece, the angelfish; and the bronze penny, the wild hog.

HINTS FOR DISABLED TRAVELERS. Senior citizens and handicapped persons are requested to notify the hotel, guest house, or cottage colony when requesting space to enable the facility to allocate a suitable room and make any special arrangements that might be required. The large hotels are best suited to handicapped persons since they have large elevators, wider doorways, more accessible bathrooms, and conveniently located public rooms. They provide wheelchairs and have sufficient hotel staff to assist the handicapped.

In addition, the Bermuda Chapter of SATH (Society for the Advancement of Travel for the Handicapped) has published a complimentary *Access Guide to Bermuda for the Handicapped Traveler,* and there are plans to update it every other year. For a copy, write SATH International, 26 Court St., Brooklyn, N.Y. 11242 (tel: 718–858–5483) or Richard M. Kitson, International Director, SATH, Box HM 449, Hamilton 5, Bermuda. His telephone number in Bermuda is 809–295–2525.

Another publication giving valuable information about facilities for the handicapped is Louise Weiss's *Access to the World: A Travel Guide for the Handicapped,* published by Facts on File (212–683–2244).

RESTAURANTS. One can dine casual or chic in Bermuda, and there is a good choice of restaurants in between. A few of the specialty restaurants and hotel dining rooms are excellent (in particular, the Newport Room in the Southhampton Princess, and Romanoff's and the Bombay Bicycle Club in Hamilton), with food, atmosphere, and service on a par with good eating in any major capital. Other restaurants can be disappointing and not worth the high cost. We suggest ordering Bermudian specialties and fish dishes that you know are fresh (or ask the waiter, if you're unsure), such as fish chowder, local fish, mussels and lobster, syllabub (a drink of cream and cider), and "Hoppin' John" (black-eyed peas and red rice), as well as rum swizzles, which are often the excuse for a party.

If you plan to dine out, advance dinner reservations are suggested. Be sure to check dress requirements. Many restaurants, especially those in hotels, require gentlement to wear a jacket and tie and women to be appropriately dressed in the evening. Dinner in the specialty restaurants can run to $50 per person (without liquor); at the medium-priced restaurants, from $30 to $40; and at the more moderate restaurants, from $20 to $30. When the gratuity is not included in the bill, an overall 10 to 15 percent is the accepted amount. (See *Dining, Wining, and Entertainment* section for a complete list of restaurants.)

SIGHTS TO SEE. There are many interesting sights to see on the island. There are historic forts *(St. Catherine, Fort Hamilton)* and churches *(St. Peter's, the Cathedral),* a good climb up *Gibbs Hill Lighthouse* for a bird's-eye view, the Botanical Gardens, dolphin acts, 17th-century houses, small museums and galleries, nature reserves, parks, and even a perfume factory. (See *What to See and Do* section.)

CLOSING TIMES. Businesses and shops are closed on the following legal holidays in 1990: New Year's Day; Good Friday (April 6); Bermuda Day (May 24); Queen's Birthday (June 18); Cup Match and Somers Day (August 2 and 3); Labour Day (September 3); Remembrance Day (November 11); Christmas Day and Boxing Day (December 25 and 26).

Businesses and shops are open from 9:30 A.M. to 5:30 P.M. and are often closed from 1 P.M. to 2 P.M. Some are closed on Thursday afternoons and all shut down on Sundays and legal holidays. Restaurants and nightspots are open from 11 A.M. weekdays, 12 noon Sundays until at least 1 A.M. and nightclubs normally keep their doors open until 3 A.M. Discotheques also keep these hours.

ELECTRICITY. Throughout the island, the electricity is 110 volts, 60 cycles AC. Appliances brought from North America do not need adapters. Those brought from the U.K. and Europe do.

MAIL, TELEPHONES, TELEGRAMS. Postal rates to the U.S. and Canada are 40 cents for airmail postcards and airmail letters. Jumbo postcards are also 40 cents. Rates to the U.K. are 30 cents for postcards, 40 cents for jumbo postcards and airmail letters per 10 grams. Direct distance dialing is available from Bermuda to the U.S., Canada, U.K., Northern Ireland, Australia, and parts of the West Indies. When dialing to Bermuda from these areas, the area code is 809, followed by either 29 or 23, and then the recently revised five-digit number. There is 24-hour cable service available and both night letter and direct full rates can apply. For overnight delivery to almost anywhere in the world, call Federal Express (295–3854), which guarantees delivery.

USEFUL ADDRESSES. Airlines: *Air Canada,* 61 Front St., Hamilton. Tel: 293–2121; *Pan American,* Front St., Hamilton. Tel: 295–8822 or 293–2480; *American Airlines,* Front St., Hamilton. Tel: 293–1420; *British Airways,* 59 Front St., Hamilton. Tel: 295–4422; *Delta Airlines,* 56 Front

St., Hamilton. Tel: 293–2000; *Eastern Airlines,* Front St., Hamilton. Tel: 292–5900;

Banks: *Bank of Bermuda,* Front St., Hamilton. Tel: 295–4000 (branches on Church St., Hamilton; St. George's; Somerset); *Bank of N.T. Butter-field & Son Ltd.,* Front St., Hamilton (branches in Somerset, St. George's, Bermudiana Rd., and at Southampton Princess Hotel); *Bermuda Provident Bank Ltd.,* Church St., Hamilton.

GETTING AROUND. There are no self-drive cars for rent in Bermuda. Therefore, visitors have a choice of bicycles, buses, carriages, ferries, taxis, or walking. Public transportation is excellent and both buses and ferries are a good way to get around. The more adventuresome will prefer motorbikes, the less active will want to take taxis everywhere.

By Cycle. WARNING. The number of accidents on mopeds isn't officially issued, but it is considerable. Most visitors aren't used to the vehicle and the few minutes of instruction across a parking lot just isn't enough.

What the Bermudians call push bikes (bicycles) and motor-assisted bikes (mopeds) are for rent throughout the island. If your hotel or cottage complex does not have an on-property livery, the nearest shop will deliver and pick up. There is no license requirement for the mopeds, but you must be 16 years of age (at least) to rent and ride them. Rates range from about $15 daily to $65 weekly for a single-person cycle, from about $25 daily to $95 weekly for a double cycle. These rates include use of helmet, lock and key, basket, full tank of gas, and instructions. Repair service is another $10 weekly. Loss of the above items can be costly, so keep everything under lock and key. It is unlawful to ride without a *strapped* safety helmet.

Visitors this season can try a Honda Lead, a sporty new two-seater scooter from Japan that seems more substantial, if more expensive ($30 a day).

Check the "Bermuda Channel" (a cable channel available in all major hotels), which offers special programs on moped safety for visitors.

Gas Stations are open from 7 A.M. to 7 P.M. Monday through Saturday. Some are closed on Sunday and have restricted hours on public holidays.

By Bus. Bermuda's pink-and-blue buses are easy to spot, especially along the principal 24-mile route between Hamilton and St. George's. Most buses operate every 15 minutes from early morning to late evening, Monday through Saturday. Bermuda is divided into 14 zones of about two miles each. The adult fare for traveling within the first three zones is $1, $2 for a longer ride. Bus stops are green-and-white-striped posts, and passengers must have the correct change ready. Don't take the bus if you're in a hurry. Between the speed limit and stops for passengers, a trip may take some time, but a bus ride can be a fun way to get to know the island at leisure. Listed below are some of the most popular destinations and the buses that will take you there:

Destination	Route Number
Aquarium	10, 11
Bermuda Museum	10, 11

Destination	Route Number
Botanical Gardens	1, 2, 7
Belmont Hotel	8
Marriott's Castle Harbour Resort	1
Crystal Caves	3, 10, 11
Devil's Hole	1, 3
Dolphin Show	10, 11
Elbow Beach	2, 7
Gibbs Hill Lighthouse	7, 8
Grotto Bay Beach Hotel	3, 10, 11
Horseshoe Bay Beach	7
Hospital	1, 2, 7
Leamington Caves	3
Club Med/St. George's Cove	10, 11
Mangrove Bay (Shops, Pubs)	7, 8
Maritime Museum (Dockyard)	8
Bermuda Perfumery	10, 11
John Smith's Bay Beach	1
Sonesta Beach Hotel	7, 8
Southampton Princess	7, 8
St. George	10, 11
Watford Bridge (for Ferry)	8

By Ferry. A wonderful way to travel from point to point is by ferry. Take the Harbour Route between Hamilton, Paget, and Warwick ($1), or try the Great Sound Route between Hamilton and Somerset Bridge ($2). Bicycles are also carried on ferries—the pedal kind go for free but motorbikes cost $2 each, provided there is room on board (avoid rush hours). One of the ship's mates will help you carry your bike on and off. Children aged 3–13 pay a flat fare of 50¢ and children under 3 travel for free. Your hotel should provide you with a ferry schedule.

By Horse-Drawn Carriages. Still popular although their number has dwindled drastically in recent years. But you will find them lined up in the shade along Front Street in Hamilton or in Flatt's Village. They are usually hired by the half-hour. The fee for two people in a single carriage is about $9.50, $12 for four people.

By Taxi. There are blue flags fluttering on the "bonnets" of 600 taxis on the island, signifying that the driver is a qualified tour guide. The men and women who earn the right to display the blue flag have passed a written examination covering all facets of their island home and a practical test on courtesy, appearance, upkeep, and driving ability. (In case you were curious, the question they are most frequently asked is why the water is so blue.) The drivers of these blue-flag taxis do not charge any more than other taxi drivers and they will impart bits and pieces of information as you creep along at 20 mph (15 mph in town). There is even one driver who quotes Tom Moore's poetry in lilting Irish! Meter rates start at $2.80 for the first mile; each subsequent mile is $1.20, and there is a 25% surcharge between midnight and 6 A.M. Taxis can be hired by the hour or by the day for sightseeing at $16 per hour. (Note: Taxi tours require a three-hour minimum.)

Some sample fares are: Hamilton to St. George, from $15 to $16; from Castle Harbour to Hamilton, about $11; from airport to Cambridge Beaches, $26–$30 (plus luggage charges); from airport to Paget, about $15; from airport to Southampton, about $21.

CRUISE TOURS. There's a choice of a Somerset cruise or a St. George's cruise. Both include a trip through the Great Sound, picnic lunch, swimming at Hawkins Island, soft drinks, rum swizzles, and calypso bands. Passengers cruise aboard the *Elizabeth* or *Georgiana* (each with a capacity of about 200 people).

The **Somerset Cruise** of about five hours operates year round, Monday through Saturday. The cruise leaves Albuoy's Point, Hamilton, at 10 A.M., with a tour of Somerset village and time for shopping. Thee's a rum swizzle party on the return trip, often with a sing-a-long. Cost is $35 per person; 292–8652 or 295–1763.

The **St. George's Cruise** is a six-hour trip, April through October. This trip runs Tuesday to Friday, and leaves Albuoy's Point, Hamilton, at 10:30 A.M., allowing time for shopping and touring in St. George. The return is merry, with a sing-a-long and rum swizzle party. Cost is $35 per person; 292–8652.

The **Reef and Wreck Adventure** of two hours, April through November, is a daily trip from 10 A.M. to 1:30 P.M. The glass-bottom boat has a capacity of 85 and takes guests from the Ferry Dock in Hamilton to the Fringe Reef. There, a commentator describes the underwater world of coral and marine life. Cost is $15 per person. Looking Glass Cruises, 236–8000.

A three- to four-hour **Snorkelling and Glass-Bottom Boat Cruise,** from mid-May through October, departs Somerset Bridge daily at 9:45 A.M. and 1:45 P.M. The glass-bottom craft *Fathom* (with a capacity of 25) cruises five miles northwest to the Perimeter Reef, where passengers see shipwrecks and marine life as the captain answers any questions. He and his crew assist snorkelers. (Children under five not permitted.) Cost is $26 per person; Pitman's Boat Tours, 234–0700.

The **Rum Swizzle Sightseeing Cruise** of one-and-a-half hours operates May to November. The boat leaves Grotto Bay Hotel dock to tour the East End, including St. David's, Ferry Reach, and the north shore. Nonstop rum drinks are included. Cost is $15 per person; Bermuda Water Sports, 293–2640 or 293–8333.

A **Sailing and Sightseeing Cruise** of three-and-a-half hours operates daily (except Sunday), departing Salt Kettle. Passengers cruise aboard the 41-foot sloop *Maid of Paget* or the 41-foot ketch *Night Watch* (both with a capacity of 16). Each vessel cruises through the small islands in Hamilton Harbour and the Great Sound; guests are often encouraged to take the helm. Rum swizzles, soft drinks, and snorkel gear are included at a swim/snorkel stop. Cost is $20 per person; Salt Kettle Boat Rentals Ltd, 296–4863 or 296–3612.

The **Cruise of Lights** from April through November takes about an hour and three-quarters, Monday to Saturday, departing at 10:30 P.M. (There's an additional Monday night cruise that leaves at 8:30 P.M.) The glass-bottom *Looking Glass,* with a capacity of 85, leaves from the ferry dock in Hamilton for a cruise around the harbor, over the sea gardens, which guests can appreciate through a lit glass-bottom. A full bar and taped music add to the enjoyment of the trip, with guest appearances by local folk guitarists. Cost is $17.50 per person; Looking Glass Cruises, 236–8000.

A **Shipwreck Dinner** is a three-night-a-week offering—Tuesday, Thursday, and Saturday. The *Reef Explorer,* with a capacity of 120, leaves the Hamilton ferry terminal at 7 P.M. for a cruise along the reefs, with a stopover for dinner at Hawkins Island, plus dancing to an upbeat band and a local show. Boat returns by 11:30 P.M. Cost is $45 per person; Bermuda Island Cruises, 295–1763 or 292–8652.

The **Sea Garden Dinner Cruise,** April through November, is a four-and-a-half-hour trip, Monday to Friday, that departs the Hamilton ferry dock at 6 P.M. There's a lit glass-bottom on board the Looking Glass (with a capacity of 85), that lets guests see the shoals along the Great Sound, where the boat docks at the Somerset Village Inn for dinner on a waterside terrace. Calypso music plays as a four-course dinner of Bermuda cuisine is served, with cocktails on board before and after the on-shore dinner. Cost is $42 per person; Looking Glass Cruises, 236–8000.

The **Submarine "Enterprise"** is the latest entry into the world at sea. Owner-captain Beau Evans is an experienced hand (he's also the owner of Looking Glass Cruises) and personally oversaw the building of this new submarine in Scotland. Cost is in the neighborhood of $50 per person. Contact Looking Glass Cruises, 236–8000.

BUS TOURS. March 1 to November 30: Combination St. George's/Harrington Sound—five hours. This tour leaves Hamilton about 10:00 A.M., Monday–Friday. Visits the caves, aquarium, museum, Devil's Hole, perfume factory, and town of St. George. Includes admissions and lunch for $30 per person. Can be booked through Penboss Associates, 295–3927.

Harrington Sound and St. George's by Bus—five hours. This tour leaves Hamilton around 10 A.M. Monday through Saturday. Visit the first capital of Bermuda, St. Peter's Church (the oldest Anglican Church in the Western Hemisphere), and the town of St. George; includes admissions and lunch. Can be booked through Butterfield Travel Ltd., 292–1510.

TAXI TOURS. Harrington Sound Tour—three hours. Visits to aquarium and museum, Devil's Hole, the caves, and perfume factory. Includes admissions only. Can be booked through: Butterfield or Penboss Associates, maximum four to taxi. Rates vary according to group size, Phone: 292–1510.

Harrington Sound St. George's—five hours. Visits to aquarium and museum, Devil's Hole, the caves, perfume factory, and town of St. George. Includes admissions only. Book through Butterfield or Penboss, maximum four to taxi. Rates vary according to group size, Phone: 292–1510.

Somerset Tour—four hours. Visits to Gibbs Hill Lighthouse, St. James Church, Cedar Souvenir Shop, Cambridge Beaches, and Linen Shop. Includes admissions and lunch in Somerset. Book through L. P. Gutteridge. Rates vary according to group size, Phone: 295–4545.

St. George's Tour—five hours. Tour of St. George's with guide. Includes admissions to the caves, Devil's Hole, aquarium and museum, and

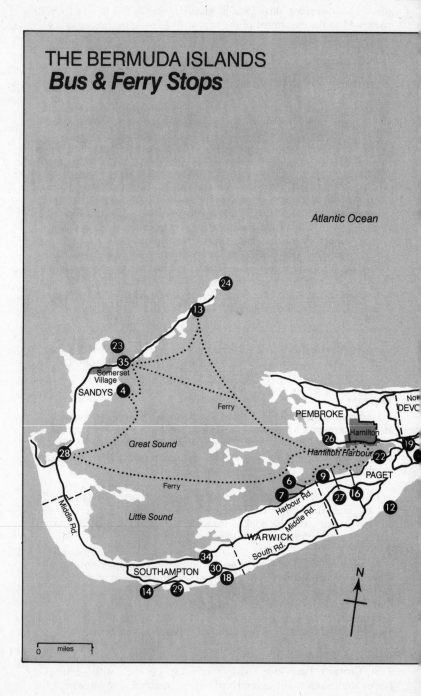

THE BERMUDA ISLANDS
Bus & Ferry Stops

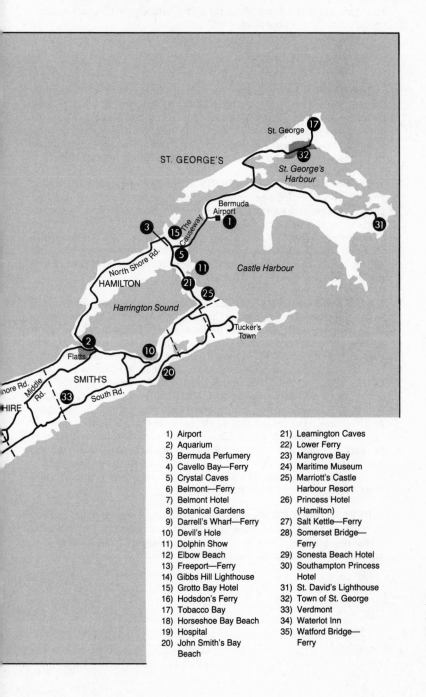

1) Airport
2) Aquarium
3) Bermuda Perfumery
4) Cavello Bay—Ferry
5) Crystal Caves
6) Belmont—Ferry
7) Belmont Hotel
8) Botanical Gardens
9) Darrell's Wharf—Ferry
10) Devil's Hole
11) Dolphin Show
12) Elbow Beach
13) Freeport—Ferry
14) Gibbs Hill Lighthouse
15) Grotto Bay Hotel
16) Hodsdon's Ferry
17) Tobacco Bay
18) Horseshoe Bay Beach
19) Hospital
20) John Smith's Bay Beach

21) Leamington Caves
22) Lower Ferry
23) Mangrove Bay
24) Maritime Museum
25) Marriott's Castle Harbour Resort
26) Princess Hotel (Hamilton)
27) Salt Kettle—Ferry
28) Somerset Bridge—Ferry
29) Sonesta Beach Hotel
30) Southampton Princess Hotel
31) St. David's Lighthouse
32) Town of St. George
33) Verdmont
34) Waterlot Inn
35) Watford Bridge—Ferry

perfume factory and lunch. Book through Gutteridge. Rates vary according to group size, Phone: 295–4545.

Nightclub Tour (groups only). Tour includes cover charge into one of Bermuda's popular nightclubs, two drinks, and gratuities. Book through Gutteridge. Rates vary according to group size, Phone: 295–4545.

SHOPPING. There are some selected buys in Bermuda for the serious shopper. Heading the list are bone china, Irish linens, Scottish tweeds, cashmere sweaters, perfumes, and liquor. There are some local handicrafts, pottery, cedar ware, and paintings by local artists. Sports gear, cameras, watches, and resort wear can also be found. Most shops take credit cards and some stores will open up a charge account in your name.

CLUBS AND ORGANIZATIONS. There are international service clubs and organizations, benevolent and patriotic associations, lodges, and special-interest and sporting organizations in Bermuda. Visitors can attend the local *Kiwanis* or *Rotary, Elks* or *Freemasons, AA, Confrerie des Chevaliers du Tastevin,* or get a letter of introduction to the *Royal Bermuda Yacht Club.* For a full list of local clubs and organizations, check with any office of the Bermuda Department of Tourism. For addresses in Bermuda, check the telephone directory.

CUSTOMS ON DEPARTURE. All passengers departing for the U.S. by air will clear U.S. Customs at the Bermuda Airport. These passengers must complete the U.S. Customs declaration and, following check-in and seat assignment from the carrier, pass through the Customs area. U.S. citizens may now, once every 30 days, take back $400 of merchandise duty-free after a stay of 48 hours. **Canadians** may take back $50 of merchandise duty-free after 48 hours once every three calendar months or $150 after seven days once every calendar year. **U.K.** citizens may bring back the following goods duty-free: 200 cigarettes, or 100 cigarillos, or 50 cigars, or 250 grams tobacco; one liter of alcohol over than 22% by volume, or two liters of alcohol of under 22% by volume, or two liters of fortified or sparkling wine and two liters of table wine; 50 grams of perfume and one-quarter liter of toilet water; plus other goods to the value of £32.

Note: U.S. citizens should check state liquor and tobacco import regulations before returning from Bermuda.

DEPARTURE TAX. Air passengers departing Bermuda must pay $10 at the time of airport check-in; children under twelve pay $5; children under two are free. The port tax for ship passengers is $40, collected in advance by the steamship company.

THE
BERMUDA
SCENE

BERMUDA'S PAST
AND PRESENT

Pink Houses and Purple Onions

Blessed with a beautiful landscape and surrounded by a turquoise sea, Britain's oldest colony and most famous resort island lies isolated in the Atlantic Ocean, more than 500 miles from the nearest land (Cape Hatteras, North Carolina). The 57,000 residents of this lovely island live on some 21-square miles of land atop a subterranean mountain and are known affectionately as "onions" after the sweet, succulent Bermuda onion that was their livelihood a century ago. Bermuda is also known for Bermuda shorts, the Bermuda Fitted Dinghy, Easter lilies, and limestone houses with "icing-on-the-cake" roofs that sparkle in the sun. These distinctive homes are all lovingly painted in pastel colors and known by their given names rather than by numbers.

On one of his many holiday excursions to the island between 1867 and his death in 1910, Mark Twain is supposed to have said, "Bermuda is Heaven but you have to go through Hell to get there!" Today's several thousand weekly visitors to Bermuda will find this remark of the American humorist only half right. It is still a "heavenly" place but one can now get there with the greatest of ease. It is less than a two-hour flight from the East Coast, nonstop across the Atlantic from London, and a leisurely 36 hours from New York by luxury cruise vessel.

Some Early Visitors

Bermuda has welcomed travelers with open arms for over three centuries. In fact, one might say that Sir George Somers and his shipwrecked party of 150 who landed in 1609 were the first visitors. They remained at the eastern end of the island (St. George's) only long enough to build two new vessels and gather provisions to continue their journey to the Jamestown Settlement in Virginia. And when they sailed away nine and a half months later, they sang such praises of the place that word reached the Virginia Company in London, which financed the first group of settlers two years later. The story of their adventure also reached William Shakespeare and inspired his play *The Tempest*. Another early "tourist" was an ailing clergyman from Massachusetts who spent seven months in Bermuda in 1663 and returned home so rejuvenated that he outlived three wives and fathered a brood of children.

One of the colony's most endearing visitors was an Irish poet named Tom Moore who spent the first four months of 1804 in St. George working in the court and writing romantic verse in his spare time. One of the many stories still told about Moore is his amorous attachment to a neighbor's wife. Many people persist in believing that the "Nea" in his poems refers to this woman, Hester Tucker, and that her firstborn is described as "the first ambrosial childe of bliss." More to fact is the time Moore did spend at "Walsingham," the beautiful 17th-century home of Samuel Trott and his family, where he immortalized the calabash tree in the front yard. The stump of the literary tree is still there and the old house became Tom Moore's Tavern for about 75 years. It is located just off Harrington Sound Road in Hamilton Parish, and reopened as a restaurant, restored to its former glory. The paneled walls and the archways on the front porch are just as they were when the poet visited.

Haven for High Society

Many Bermudians feel that tourism as a serious business began in the winter of 1883 with the arrival of Princess Louise, daughter of Queen Victoria, who fled the cold and wintry climate of Canada where her husband was the governor-general. The residents of this crown colony had never seen a real-live princess and, no doubt, her visit did receive much attention in the press of the English-speaking world. It also inspired the opening of the colony's first hotel, the Princess Hotel in Hamilton, which provided all the amenities the rich and playful needed, including direct telephones to the city. This was the beginning of a trend that would last until World War II. During the winter months, the wealthy began to come to Bermuda for "the season," together with ladies' maids and steamer trunks full of tea-dance dresses. They drank lots of tea, played croquet or tennis, and visited their friends via horse-drawn carriages. Tennis was *le sport* and came to Bermuda as early as 1873—the first tennis tournament in the Western Hemisphere took place here in 1877. (A young Bermudian lady, Miss Mary Outerbridge, introduced the game to the United States in 1874 by taking her equipment and book of rules to the Staten Island Cricket Club in New York.)

Soon, larger and newer hotels sprang up around the island and the "guest house" concept was born. Many visitors then (and now) wouldn't stay in anything else because they said this captures "the real" Bermuda. In the 1920s, the exclusive Mid-Ocean Club in Tucker's Town was founded, with a golf course that equaled any in the world. Golf soon became *le sport.*

Bermuda was especially popular during the Roaring Twenties because it was still quaint but civilized and alcohol was legal. During the Prohibition years in the U.S., those that could afford it did their drinking aboard steamships going back and forth to the island. The first commercial passenger flights between New York and Bermuda were offered in the late 1930s, while as many as six different steamship lines scheduled weekly sailings. As the island's popularity as a resort increased, visitors arrived year-round, not just for "the season," to fill the hotels, cottages, and guest houses and to travel about by the new narrow gauge railway between Hamilton and St. George's, as undependable as it was charming.

A New Era

But alas, with the advent of World War II, the large cruise vessels in Hamilton Harbour were painted a dull gray and sent on more somber missions. Bermuda lost the "beautiful people" for a few years, but the slack was taken up with British and American forces. The U.S. was given a 99-year lease on a square mile of land that surrounds the airport. The Americans introduced motorized vehicles to the island. Through it all, though, the colony hung tenaciously to her charm, and the tourists flocked back after the war as fast as they had fled.

Today, the island receives over half a million visitors a year. They come to play golf or tennis on the grounds of large resort hotels, lounge around cottage colonies and beaches, stay in small guest houses, or take housekeeping apartments with their families. Bermuda has subtly adapted to her visitors and now offers something for everyone. While honeymooners may pick the traditional months of June or September, couples come anytime to celebrate their anniversaries. Golfers may be wooed during the winter months, but the greens and fairways are inviting year-round. And there is plenty to do to keep the whole family busy. After a morning at the beach, young ones can visit maritime and historical museums, see dolphins that dance, explore underground caves, and have a tug of war with a turtle.

Traditions

Bermudians treasure their traditions and like to share them with visitors—both the colonial pomp they have inherited and the local ceremonies they developed. The justices still wear powdered wigs as they impart British law but can be found on the evening circuit in Bermuda shorts. The crown-appointed governor appears in full plumage on special occasions. He journeys to St. George every spring to collect the annual rent of one peppercorn (presented on a velvet pillow) for the old State House, throws a garden party in June to celebrate the Queen's official birthday, and hitches up a pair of fine horses to the state landau to open Parliament in the fall.

Christmastime in Bermuda traditionally means passing around the cassava pie, made from a recipe handed down for 300 years, and running out to join the Gombey Dancers who wend their way along the narrow lanes during the holiday period. The local wedding tradition features a horse-drawn carriage for the bride and groom and separate wedding cakes. The groom has a single layer cake covered with gold leaf while the bride cuts a three-tiered silver cake topped with a cedar sapling. This custom, adapted from the Dutch, dictates that the couple plant the sapling on their wedding day (hopefully in front of their new home). If it grows straight and strong, so will their marriage. Sports are another local tradition. Bermudians all flock to the beaches on Bermuda Day (May 24, 1990), the official opening of the swimming season. Sailing, soccer, and cricket are favorite pastimes and the annual Cup Match between the island's two cricket teams is an official holiday.

Bermuda Shorts

As reflected by their dress, Bermudians live a casual life that has a tinge of quiet elegance to it. During the winter months, men wear tartans, light tweeds, and pullovers. From May to November, the famous Bermuda shorts are de rigueur. Shorts that stopped just above the knee and worn with long socks that were turned over just below the knee were introduced to the island in the early 1900s by members of the British military. The early styles were dull gray and khaki, belted and baggy, but they kept the troops cool in the midday sun.

By the 1920s, tailors along Front Street were making streamlined versions and local Hamilton merchants were wearing the shorts, along with knee socks, tie and jacket, during the working day—but never to dinner or church. Bermuda shorts were born. But there were always strict rules—the proper length was two to four inches above the knees, and there was a time in the 1950s when local police handed out "green tickets" to wearers of shorts that were "too short." Although the official Bermuda shorts season for the police force is May to November, many local gentlemen wear them year-round. They even wear them with evening dress in the summer. Bermuda shorts have become their trademark.

Architecture

Bermuda has its own style of architecture, developed as early as 1620 when Governor Moore ordered the building of a proper State House. Because wooden structures with raffia roofs did not withstand the ravages of storms, Moore ordered a simple and functional building of native stone with thick walls, low ceilings, and a flat roof. The flat roof was the governor's only error. Not only did it always leak, it couldn't catch the precious rain, which was the island's only source of pure water. Bermudians have wisely emulated their ancestors' functional design and it is this uniformity of construction featuring stone walls and stepped roofs that makes for a unique style. Highly polished cedar doors and floors, large fireplaces that served a double purpose (cooking and heating), and "tray" ceilings have been an integral part of the Bermudian home for three centuries.

These buildings were all made of native Bermudian coral, an aeolian limestone quarried by hand and cut into rectangular blocks, then plastered on both sides to prevent deterioration. When put into place, the blocks were given several coats of whitewash. These blocks were actually quarried from the backyard of the newly designated structure, and the excavation was utilized as a storage tank for fresh water. The building's roof of limestone slabs was pitched so rain water could be channeled down through stone gutters to the storage tank. Today, tanks are underground and have flat roofs of reinforced concrete. To keep the rain water fresh and pure, a lime wash was applied regularly to the roof (a nontoxic white paint is now used). It is this "icing-on-the-cake" roof that is so distinctively Bermudian. Modern houses are also built of cement block and stucco, but the construction is the same. Over the years, their exterior walls have been painted bright Bermuda pink, pumpkin orange, pastel blue, green, or yellow.

Inside, native cedar has been used for centuries for the beams, floors, furniture, door, and window frames. This cedar, now practically extinct after a blight in the 1940s, adapts well to woodworking, adds a special warmth to the structure, and lasts forever (the early colonists used this cedar for shipbuilding). Other charming features of a typical Bermudian home were the "welcoming arms" stairway to the front door (built wider at the bottom than at the top to welcome visitors), and the "tray" ceilings devised to counteract the extreme height of the roof and collect heat from the rooms. As the term suggests, the ceilings are shaped like the inside of an upside down tea tray.

Some of the older homes still have a separate buttery, or ice house, a miniature of the larger building topped with a decorative sphere on its roof. "Slave walls," or dry stone walls built by former slaves, are also seen. Bermudians treated their slaves relatively well and rarely traded them once they became part of the family. They housed them either in the basement of the family home or in a separate dwelling on the same property.

Every spring sometime between mid-March and mid-May, private Bermudian homes and gardens are open to the public during an annual tour sponsored by the Garden Club of Bermuda. A different set of three homes is open each Wednesday over a four-week period. The properties chosen are large and small, with a good cross-section of the new and old. Visitors on the tour will notice that Bermuda houses do not have numbers, but have been bestowed with names such as Open Hearth, Orange Grove, Cedar Hill, Salt Winds, and Heron's Nest.

At least two historic houses are open to visitors year-round. The 17th-century mansion "Verdmont" (Collector's Hill, Smith's Parish) was built between 1616 and 1662 by Captain William Sayle, twice governor of the island. The cedar staircase in the house is considered to be the finest in Bermuda, and the windows still have most of their original panes.

The Tucker House (Water Street, St. George) was the home of Henry Tucker, whose father, Colonel Tucker of Southampton, led the conspiracy to give gunpowder to the American colonies in exchange for food. It is a fine example of a mid-18th-century house. It is full of beautiful, old family furniture, much of it presented by Robert Tucker of Baltimore, who lived to be 102. Some of the Tucker sons were educated at William and Mary College and remained in the United States. Thomas Tudor Tucker, brother of Henry, became a treasurer of the U.S.

Gombey Dancers

A local tradition is the appearance of the Gombey dancers on all major holidays, including Boxing Day (December 26), New Year's Day, and during Heritage month (May). They sing and dance their way around the island like pied pipers, bringing many of the children along with them in a carnival-like atmosphere. The Gombeys emerged during the slavery days in Bermuda, with music and rhythm brought from Africa and the West Indies. The skin-covered drum the original dancers used was called "gombey," which means rhythm.

The dancers wear colorful costumes with beads, sequins, fringe, and tassels. They wear high headdresses topped with feathers and covered with tiny mirrors that reflect and distort the scenes around them as they move. Grotesque masks enhance their frenzied, winding movement. Coins are traditionally thrown at their feet to make them move faster. They are accompanied only by drummers, most of whom do not read music and play simply by ear and instinct.

Gombey dancing is a Christmas custom as important as the evergreen trees imported from North America, the poinsettias blooming wild all over the island, and cassava pie, a dish made from a 300-year-old recipe that calls for spiced cassava dough and a filling of beef, pork, and chicken.

Geography

Bermuda is a tiny dot on any world map, remote from the nearest land. The country consists of about 150 islands, the seven largest connected by bridges and causeways and arranged in the shape of a giant fish hook. From east to west, Bermuda is about 22 miles long with a maximum width of less than two miles, forming a land area of 20.59 square miles. Geologists say that this land area is perched on the summit of a submarine mountain that rises 15,000 feet from the bottom of the sea, and was created some 100 million years ago by a volcano. The islands are surrounded by coral reefs that have protected them from unwanted invaders, as well as from natural erosion.

Bermuda has a mild, subtropical climate because the Gulf Stream tempers the wintry winds that sweep across the Atlantic from west and north. The average yearly temperature is 70 degrees F. (21 degrees C.) and annual rainfall is 1,270 mm (50 inches), spread evenly over the 12 months. The sun shines an average of seven hours per day, 351 days a year. However, because Bermuda is entirely surrounded by water, the weather on any given day can range from intense solar heat to cool, gusty winds and heavy rain squalls. (The visitor must be prepared for anything!)

Winters can be quite cold, and jackets are definitely required. It's a good time for active sports such as golf or tennis. Spring comes early to the island, along with oleander, hibiscus, and bougainvillea that bloom along every roadside. The days are warm from late spring through early fall, and water sports prevail as favorite pastimes for both residents and visitors.

Early History

Credit for discovery of the islands in 1503 is given to Spanish navigator Juan de Bermudez, who gave the area his name. A map published in the *Legatio Babylonica* in 1511 includes an island called "La Bermuda." But the Spanish never attempted to settle the area and referred to it as "Isles of the Devil." They said that it was inhabited by bad spirits who lured ships to their graveyard among the treacherous reefs. Another historical source says that in 1515, a Gonzales Ferdinando d'Oviedo tried to land pigs on the islands to provide food for the crews of ships that came near or were wrecked along the reefs.

So Bermuda was uninhabited when 150 passengers aboard the 300-ton *Sea Venture* were shipwrecked off what is now St. Catherine's Beach in 1609 and spent almost a year on the eastern end of the island. The *Sea Venture* was the flagship of a nine-vessel fleet that set sail from Plymouth, England, on June 2, 1609, to carry colonists and provisions to the new Jamestown Settlement in Virginia. Among the prominent passengers on board sent by the Jamestown Company were: Sir George Somers, admiral of the fleet; Sir Thomas Gates, deputy governor of Jamestown; his aide, William Strachey; and John Rolfe, who later married the Indian Princess Pocahontas and made American history books.

After almost two months at sea, the *Sea Venture* ran into a hurricane that threw her off course from the rest of the fleet. For three days the vessel tossed, filling with water. Just as the passengers had given up hope of keeping her afloat, land was sighted. Sir George ordered the vessel landward but she ran aground on a reef at the eastern end of Bermuda. Through the wisdom of their two leaders, all 150 passengers and most of their provisions were landed safely in small boats on the beach below St. Catherine's Point.

During their stay, the men of the party built two new ships, the *Deliverance* and *Patience,* from the salvaged wreck of the *Sea Venture* and the tall, strong cedars they found, while the women gathered food. By the second week in May 1610, the castaways were prepared to continue their journey and sailed for Jamestown, leaving two men behind by their own preference. One was a convicted murderer. The other, Christopher Carter, is frequently called Bermuda's first settler.

Sir George and his party arrived in Jamestown within two weeks and found the small settlement sick and starving. He offered to return to Bermuda for more food, and there he died of exhaustion. His nephew, Matthew Somers, buried the heart of Sir George near their original landing site of 1609 and carried the body back to England aboard the *Patience* (disregarding the needs of Jamestown).

Soon, fascinating tales of the "Somers Islands" were the talk of London and the Virginia Company. A letter describing the adventure in detail was sent from Jamestown by William Strachey to the Countess of Bedford, who shared it with members of the Virginia Company. These included the Earl of Southampton, a patron of William Shakespeare, who based his idyllic play *The Tempest* on the Bermuda happening.

Two years later, some fifty-odd settlers, sponsored by the Virginia Company, sailed into the harbor at the eastern end of Bermuda and founded the town of St. George, in honor of Sir George Somers and St. George, the patron saint of England. It was the capital of Bermuda for 203 years. By 1616, the 21-square-mile land was surveyed and divided into eight large tribes, each one named after a member of the company (now called the Bermuda Company), and bounded by a path just wide enough to roll a barrel along. These tribes are the parishes we know today and the tribe roads are still in existence. The parishes are Sandys, Southampton, Warwick, Paget, Pembroke, Devonshire, Smith's, Hamilton, and St. George's, which was later added to the original eight.

In 1620, the newly appointed Governor Butler convened Bermuda's first Parliament in St. Peter's Church (the site of the oldest Anglican church in the Western Hemisphere in continuous use) and set about building a proper State House. His foresight in constructing the building entirely of native limestone, to withstand the ravages of storms as well as to save the already dwindling supply of indigenous cedar, set the example for traditional Bermudian architecture. The State House is Bermuda's oldest building but has not been in official use since the capital moved to Hamilton in 1815. It is in trust to the Masonic Lodge for an annual rent of one peppercorn, which is paid in a colorful ceremony every April.

Toward the end of the 17th century, Bermuda officially became a royal colony, governed by the British monarch. The islanders supported themselves through shipbuilding, trading salt from the Turks Islands, slaves from Africa and the West Indies, whaling, and pirating. Of all these trades, piracy was the most lucrative. On the sea, Bermudians were a tough lot to surpass. The coffers of St. George were full of foreign coins either from far-flung sailings or from the ships wrecked along the island reefs. Bermuda became so rich from piracy that agriculture was neglected and the islands were soon dependent upon their American cousins for most of their food supply. Islanders bartered food for salt brought up from the Turks Islands.

Ties That Bind

The link that was established between the Bermuda Islands, American colonies, and Great Britain in 1609 grew stronger during the early history of both colonies and, indeed, has never been broken. When the "shot heard 'round the world" was fired on the village green in Concord, Massachusetts, in 1775, the Bermudians attempted to remain neutral, considering the confrontation between their American cousins and the Mother Country a private spat. But soon the islanders were bitterly divided over the American Revolution, because many of them had families and close connections in the colonies, especially Virginia. While the Bermudians as a whole had no intention of cutting their ties with the Mother Country, they realized that they had to be at peace with the Americans or they faced starvation.

In the summer of 1775, Colonel Henry Tucker (whose son was a student at William and Mary College in Williamsburg, Virginia) appeared before the Continental Congress to plead for the continuation of trading salt for food, but the Americans turned down the request because they wanted gunpowder—the large stock of gunpowder that was stored on the island. General Washington wrote to the citizens of Bermuda from his camp outside Boston, begging them to sell the gunpowder to his army in exchange for a continuation of friendship and provisions. However, before his letter even had time to reach the island, a small group of Bermudians took matters into their own hands. In the heat of a mid-August night, they removed the entire store of gunpowder and relayed it to two American warships anchored outside St. George's harbor. (The names of those involved are still spoken in whispers, but there is no doubt that the Tucker family was behind the scheme.) Although the governor was furious when he found out, Bermuda continued to be supplied with food throughout the war.

During the War of 1812, Bermuda became an active base for the Royal Navy and her fine harbors a repository for captured American warships. *The President,* one of the vessels brought in, was the victim of the last sea battle in January 1815. Aboard *The President* was a wounded young seaman named Richard Sutherland Dale. He soon died and was buried in St. Peter's graveyard. His tombstone is inscribed with the gratitude of his parents for the tender care he received from the citizens of St. George's.

Slavery was abolished in Bermuda in 1834, but most of the island favored the southern Confederacy during the American Civil War, especially the area around St. George. Blockade running was the name of the game during this war, and the warehouses of St. George were soon full of guns for the Confederate Army and cotton bound for Europe. But fast riches did not last, and by 1865, the end of the war, the townsfolk were in debt with unsold rotten goods in the warehouses.

One can still find the remnants of this brief glory. The Confederate Museum, in the very building where much of the wartime operations took place, is full of memorabilia of the "gilded" days of the 1860s. Local residents will also point out Barber's Alley, which adjoins the kitchen of the Tucker home, where a former South Carolina slave named Joseph Hayne Rainey set up a barber shop. Rainey and his wife fled to Bermuda prior to the Civil War but returned to South Carolina in 1865, where he became the first black elected to the U.S. House of Representatives.

Spy Story

During World War II, the colony played her most fascinating role. The story is best told in William Stevenson's *A Man Called Intrepid,* an exciting account of the secret diplomacy and intelligence operations of the allied powers. According to Stevenson, there were some 1,200 British experts working in the cellars of the pink Hamilton Princess Hotel, intercepting mail and messages between the United States and the Continent. These men and women, recruited in England, were trained to decipher microdot messages sent by German spies in ordinary letters. Most of the messages were in mail carried on the New York/Europe route, aboard planes that landed in Bermuda "to refuel." While passengers and crew were treated to tea, the experts could examine and reseal as many as 200,000 pieces of mail and cargo. Stevenson reports that the majority of these "trappers" were women with "long ears, sharp eyes, and well-turned ankles." For some reason, the prettier the ankle, the better a woman was at the job of detection.

In addition to exposing German spies in the U.S., the trappers saved a collection of 270 Impressionist paintings stolen by the Nazis in France. The paintings were taken off a ship in Bermuda harbor, stored in a local bank vault, and returned to their astonished rightful owner at the end of the war. Tracking enemy U-boats was another activity on the island. A German submarine became a secret prize of the war and was put into immediate use as a training vessel for both the Royal and U.S. navies.

During World War II, Prime Minister Winston Churchill made one of several visits to Bermuda, this one in earnest. He flew in and out in January 1942 on a Pan Am Clipper and addressed the Bermuda Assembly in between. He was so impressed with the atmosphere on the island that in 1953, he suggested that the Big Three hold their summit meeting at the

Mid-Ocean Club, and Eisenhower, Churchill, and French Premier Laniel gathered there. Eisenhower returned in 1957 to confer with Prime Minister Macmillan. In 1961, Macmillan joined with President Kennedy for the Bermuda Conference, and President Nixon and Prime Minister Edward Heath met there in 1971.

After almost 200 years in Bermuda, the British withdrew their forces in 1957, but the U.S. Naval Air Station's rent-free lease at Kindley Field runs through the year 2040. In addition, one of the most important stations in the space-tracking network of the National Aeronautics and Space Administration operates on Cooper's Island at Bermuda's eastern end. Locally, Bermuda has her own army, the Bermuda Regiment, with a strength of approximately 450 part-time soldiers.

Government

Bermuda's government passed to the crown in 1684. Her constitution remained relatively unchanged until 1968, when Bermudians were given a greater say in the conduct of local affairs, superseding the constitution of 1888. The Bermuda government is composed of a crown-appointed governor, a premier and his cabinet, the House of Assembly, and the Senate.

The Cabinet: This body of 12 is headed by the premier, who is elected by members of his party. Each member of the Cabinet is appointed by the premier and is assigned an area of government operations. The various ministries include health and social services, tourism, transportation, agriculture, immigration, education, finance, legislative, industry, and technology.

House of Assembly: The five-year elected body of government is composed of 40 MPs, or Members of Parliament. The island is divided into 20 electoral districts, four for Pembroke Parish and two for each of the other eight parishes. The ruling political party is the United Bermuda Party, while the opposition is called the Progressive Labour Party. A third, smaller party, the National Liberal Party (NLP), has been recently established. The election of 1968 was the first held in Bermuda under a party system and the first in which all people over the age of 21 were eligible to register to vote and cast a ballot.

The Senate: Also known as the upper house of Parliament. There are 11 members of the Senate, which approves bills before the governor signs them into statute. Five of the members are appointed on the advice of the premier, three on the advice of the opposition leader, and three by the governor himself.

Judicial responsibility falls to the Supreme Court, which is headed by a crown-appointed chief justice. (The present chief justice, appointed by Queen Elizabeth, is a distinguished black Bermudian.) The judges impart Bermudian law in traditional robes and wigs. There is also an appeal court and two lower courts.

Economics

In the absence of nearly all forms of direct taxation, the government of Bermuda obtains most of its revenues from the duty on all imported goods for visitors and residents. There is no local income tax, but a small land tax was instituted in 1967 to increase revenue. Visitors will also find a 6 percent room tax and one of the highest airport taxes in the world ($10 per person). Children under 12 pay $5 on airport departure. Port taxes for cruise passengers are also very steep, at $40, but this amount is prepaid in the overall cruise package price.

There is no doubt that the people of Bermuda enjoy a high standard of living, with no personal income tax, practically no unemployment, and no national debt. But the cost of living is also high, even though the government has managed to keep inflation to a modest 5 percent. A home can sell for as high as $3 million (a non-Bermudian may not purchase one for less than $350,000), a small dresser for the bedroom can run up to $700 after import duties, and the food and sundries in the supermarkets, all imported, are costly.

There is no heavy industry in Bermuda, and the economy is now based on tourism and on companies that set up headquarters on the island to avoid heavy taxation and complicated laws at home. These British, American, and Canadian companies pay some form of taxation to the Bermuda government but are "exempt" from others. Some of them are no more than a file in a drawer, but others, like Bacardi International, have built elegant headquarters and hired many local residents. Still, 65 cents of every dollar spent in Bermuda comes from tourism.

There are now over 100 hotels, cottage colonies, housekeeping apartments, and guest houses in Bermuda. Tourism is heavily controlled by the government, with laws designed to save local jobs (should the market fall) as well as to preserve tourist facilities. There is a moratorium on building new hotels, and only certain government-appointed wholesalers are permitted to package vacation programs to Bermuda. Both scheduled aircraft and a limited number of charter flights are allowed to bring in visitors, and only a certain number of cruise vessels can dock at any given time.

There are now three ports of call for cruise ships to Bermuda: the city port of Hamilton; St. George at the eastern end of the island; and most recently, the Dockyard, on the western tip of Bermuda. There's a double blessing here—passengers see several Bermuda stops, and not each other, since stops are staggered.

Visitors will only return again and again as long as there are no internal problems. The question of independence raises hot debate on the island. Loyalists argue that the island doesn't need independence and can't afford it. Separatists argue that independence is needed. But all the colony's 57,000 people, of whom approximately 35,000 are black, argue in a spirit of patriotism toward the island-nation that they share.

"Whither the Fates lead us" (Quo Fata Ferunt) has been the motto of Bermudians since 1615 and Bermudians have done well by the fates so far. There is no doubt that with all Bermudians working together, this beautiful island will remain steady in an unsteady world.

EXPLORING BERMUDA

Clean Air, Crystal Water, and Fragrant Flowers

While exploring the 21 square miles of this beautiful island in the Atlantic, you'll be treated to breathtaking views of the sea and shore and to the sight of the colorful, subtropical flowers and plants that grace every byway. Oleander and hibiscus hedges dominate the scenery, while palm trees and cacti provide a lush background. On some of the narrower lanes, the flora is so prolific that it almost forms a ceiling for you to pass under. Indeed, a sunny day in Bermuda is meant for chugging along the charming roads of the island, breathing in the fresh and fragrant air.

The best way to explore Bermuda is via mopeds or, as the Bermudians say, motor-assisted cycles. Both single cycles and two-seaters are available for rent at cycle liveries everywhere for the hour, the day, the week, or longer. They are a very tricky mode of transportation, even if you obey the speed limit and wear your safety helmet at all times. The bigger and sturdier, recently introduced Honda Lido scooters could prove to be a safer mode of travel. However, local cars and trucks do not always watch out for visitors, so be careful. Stay off the roads at night and in rainy weather.

Bermuda's roads are narrow and winding—most of them were laid out originally for pedal bicycles (push bikes) and horse-drawn vehicles. The Tribe Roads, designed in 1616 as boundaries between the parishes, are much as they were in the 17th century and are really no more than narrow paths. Since 1946, when automobiles officially arrived on the island, the speed limit has been set at 20 mph on open roads and 15 mph in the town of St. George's and the city of Hamilton.

You can't get lost in Bermuda (at least not very) because the island is only one-and-a-half miles at its widest point and you're never too far from one of the main arteries that run east and west. These are the North Shore Road, South Shore Road, and Middle Road. A number of smaller roads run alongside them and crisscross them at regular intervals. Every convenience is available for visitors who plan to cycle about. There are plenty of filling stations (even though one can do the entire island and back on a single tank of gas), and complimentary maps are available at every Visitor's Bureau, hotel desk, and cycle livery. The local ferries will carry your cycle (provided there is room) for about $2 and the mates help you carry it on and off.

Indeed, a perfect day's excursion is to take the ferry across the Great Sound to Somerset Bridge and cycle about from there. Somerset Bridge, which links the village to the main island of Bermuda, is considered the world's smallest drawbridge. It has an 18-inch draw that opens for the masts of sailboats. In addition to exploring the village of Somerset, you can have a swim on Long Bay on the northwest coast or catch a glass-bottom boat trip from Mangrove Bay over to the reefs, with a stop for snorkeling and swimming along the way. Following lunch at one of the funny local inns, take a drive out to Land's End, Ireland Island, for a visit to the Maritime Museum and Royal Keepyard. On the way back to Somerset Bridge for the return ferry, don't forget to stop and rest on the grassy slopes of Fort Scaur, which offers a wonderful view of the Great Sound. Chat with the caretaker and sign the guest book (he will appreciate it).

At least one day should be spent on St. George's Island, which has more attractions per square foot than any other site in Bermuda. Wandering through the crooked streets and alleys with their funny names (Featherbed Alley, Petticoat Lane, Barber's Alley, Old Maid's Lane), you have the chance to explore 380 years of history that intertwines Bermuda, the United Kingdom, and North America. Two of the island's five restored forts and one of its two lighthouses are on St. George's, as are superb beaches and 18th-century buildings that are homes, quaint shops, and inns.

Returning to the main island, you can stop off at a perfume factory, two limestone caverns that are open to the public, a bird sanctuary, and Devil's Hole where fish, turtles, and sharks swim side by side. Riding along the South Shore Road offers a view of some of the most beautiful beaches in the world and a six-mile stretch of reef, known as The Boilers because the surf constantly breaks along its top. High above is the Gibbs Hill Lighthouse. From its height of 362 feet above sea level, visitors have a spectacular sight of the Great Sound and the small islands it encompasses.

Cycling in the city of Hamilton is no problem. There is plenty of parking available along the harbor under the same trees that provide shelter for the few remaining horse-and-carriage operators. In fact, let your cycle rest a bit and take a carriage ride around the town. Bermuda has embraced the modern world, but her style and dignity have not changed.

Of course, there are other ways to explore Bermuda, but one has to rely on either taxis or public transportation. There are no cars for rent, but there are exactly 600 taxis on the island, of which 400 have a blue flag on the hood (or bonnet as Bermudians say), which means that the driver is a qualified tour guide. He or she has taken a stiff written examination, as well as a practical test on courtesy and driving ability. It does not cost any more to take a "blue flag" taxi, so if you feel like chatting a bit and asking a few questions on what you've seen around the island, be sure to catch one. All taxis can be hired by the hour or the day for sightseeing, and the drivers will help you plan an interesting (and convenient) itinerary.

Local buses are another easy way to sightsee. Bus stops are well marked along the main roads. Passengers must have the correct change ($1 for the first 3 zones, $2 for a longer ride). The courteous bus driver will tell you how much to put into the till and let you know when he has reached your destination. Buses are a friendly way to explore, and you will meet some interesting people en route, both locals and visitors.

But no one should leave Bermuda without exploring, at least once, by ferry. Ferries leave every few minutes from Hamilton for Paget, Warwick, and Somerset. This is an island resort that should be seen by water, and short of having one's own private yacht, the ferry is a good substitute. It is also one of the few bargains left—$1 one way to Paget or Warwick and $2 one way to Somerset.

Guests in Paget or Warwick hotels can easily take the ferry to Hamilton for a day's shopping and sightseeing. Newstead is a short walk from the Hodsdon's Landing (10-minute ride to Hamilton); Glencoe—one of our favorites—is a five-minute walk from Salt Kettle; the Inverurie Hotel is next to Darrell's Wharf; and the Belmont Hotel is a stiff climb up the hill from the Belmont dock. The ferries run frequently.

The two major ferry stops on Somerset Island are Somerset Bridge and Watford Bridge. If you are taking a cycle along, get off at the former and catch the ferry from the latter point at the end of the day. (It's all the same price.) The stop for trips to the Dockyard is at Freeport on Ireland Island.

These ferries are romantic because the water is a vivid blue and the scenery so lively, with pastel houses climbing up and down the hillsides. They are also a reminder of how the early settlers traveled around the island, although not in such luxury. It's doubtful that they had a closed compartment in which to take refuge from wind and rain.

Sandys Parish

The charming village of Somerset is the focal point of Sandys Parish, which encompasses the islands of Somerset, Boaz, and Ireland north and south. The parish is named after Sir Edwin Sandys, another of the large shareholders in the original Bermuda Company. Somerset honors Sir George Somers, the valiant admiral of the *Sea Venture*. This whole area at the western end of the Bermuda chain is a favorite with visitors, who enjoy its gentle charm, quiet lanes, and sheltered coves. The area boasts two fine harbors, a handsome parish church, a fort built at the Duke of Wellington's suggestion, two nature reserves, a maritime museum, and the smallest drawbridge in the world.

Sandys begins at the end of the main island, just after the Port Royal Golf Course near the U.S. Naval Air Station Annex. It is bisected by Middle Road, which ends at Somerset Bridge. This tiny bridge links the main island with Somerset and has a draw of 18 inches, just enough to let through the mast of a small sailing vessel. This drawbridge crosses an inlet between Ely's Harbour and the Great Sound, and from here one can pick up an oleander-lined byway that follows the old railroad tracks into the village of Somerset. (The narrow-gauge railroad that ran between Somerset and St. George's was taken up when automobiles arrived on the island and shipped to Guyana in 1948.)

Ely's Harbour, now full of small pleasure craft bobbing on their buoys, was important to the early traders of Bermuda since it provided a quick shelter from sudden storms at sea. It was also a smuggler's haven. Overlooking it on the western shore of Sandys is Wreck Hill, the site of early fortifications. The Scaur Lodge property overlooks the harbor and Scaur Bay, where cathedral rocks form interesting shapes. Overlooking the Great Sound is Fort Scaur, another of the fortifications built under the military defense scheme of the Duke of Wellington. Built into the hilltop, its series of bunkers and tunnels are surrounded by dry moats. The whole grassy area has been equipped with picnic tables. The fort's caretaker welcomes visitors and enjoys treating them to a personal tour, all the time imparting local history. Sandys' citizens have always had their own strong minds and rarely agreed with the rest of the colony on which side they should take during outside conflicts. During the American Civil War, for example, this area heavily supported the North and its Union army.

More local history can be found in the parish church of St. James, one of the loveliest churches on the island. No one knows for certain when the original church on this site was built, but it was probably made of wood and destroyed by a hurricane. Part of the present structure was built in 1789, with the north and south aisles added in 1836. A century later, the church was struck by lightning and the spire fell perpendicularly into the center aisle. The present spire, designed by a local architect, is floodlit at night to show off its perfectly proportioned beauty. In addition to the polished cedar doors and interior of the church, one is impressed by the bright and happy feeling within the structure. The long driveway from the main road is lined with whitewashed graves, all glistening in the brilliant sunshine.

On both sides of Somerset Island are lovely bays and beaches for exploring and swimming. Traveling along the West Side Road, you pass Church Bay (with St. James Church on the hill above), Margaret's Bay, and down to Daniel's Head, where there is a station for the Canadian Armed Forces. In this area overlooking Long Bay is also Skeeter's Corner, where an interesting murder took place last century. It seems that a local man named Skeeters killed his wife one evening because she talked too much. He tied her body to a boulder and dropped her in the bay. The neighbors were suspicious and recovered the body, and Mr. Skeeters was convicted and executed. But this hairy tale should not detract from one's enjoyment of Long Bay, which has some beautiful beaches.

Around the corner is Mangrove Bay, a bustling little area with Cambridge Beaches, Bermuda's oldest cottage colony, at one end. From Mangrove Bay wharf, one can take sightseeing boats out to the reefs for snorkeling and swimming or embark on fishing and sailing adventures. The bay got its name from the Mangrove trees that used to line the shore but, alas, do so no more.

Within the village of Somerset, there are charming shops and inns, as well as quiet lanes down which to cycle or wander. It is a pleasant town that always seems just about to take a siesta (or is waking up from one).

If you prefer to travel by ferry, the Watford Bridge dock is just down the road and within easy walking distance of such local spots as the Loyalty Inn, The Old Market, Il Palio Italian restaurant, Sandys Souvenir Shop, and Ye Village Corner. A ten-minute walk along Somerset Road brings you to one of the properties belonging to the Bermuda National Trust, Springfield, and the Gilbert Nature Reserve.

Springfield is an old plantation home owned by the Gilbert family from 1700 to 1973, when it was acquired by the Trust in conjunction with the Audubon Society. The property encompasses five acres of unspoiled woodland, open space, and planting land that adjoins an old plantation home. Known as Springfield, the building, with courtyard, separate kitchen, buttery, and slave quarters, is interesting as an early 18th-century Bermudian structure. The finest rooms in the house are used as the Somerset branch of the Bermuda Library and unfortunately are only open on Mondays, Wednesdays, and Saturdays, but the grounds are open daily.

From the center of town, go on to Sugar Cane Point and cross Watford Bridge to Watford, Boaz, and Ireland islands. This area extends all the way to Land's End and the Royal dockyard. Shipbuilding was the major source of income for this area and much of the work was done by convicts brought out from England and kept in close quarters on board old frigates. Sandys' people were proud of their dockyard but were often worried about what would happen to the economy if shipbuilding ceased to be a major world enterprise. In the early years of this century, as Cambridge Beaches opened its doors to visitors, they found out that tourism would be the economic replacement.

The area utilized on Ireland Island North was the only fully planned dockyard in the British Empire and was under control of the Royal Navy from 1837. Royal naval forces were much in evidence around the colony during the War of 1812, when campaigns such as the burning of Washington in 1814 were operated from Bermuda. A fortress was constructed around the dockyard by convicts and a Commissioner's House was built on a hill overlooking the entire area. Guns were placed around the entire embankment. But the munitions were never needed and by the 1920s, the defenses were abandoned. This inner fortification is known as the "Keepyard" and is now of interest to visitors to the Maritime Museum.

As moats were known to exist in the Keepyard, the museum's director began to excavate the area a few years ago and discovered some fine old buoys. It appears that a buoy shop was once located here, and the museum is now putting together a fine collection of mid-19th-century buoys—one of the best in the world.

This is a splendid place, an outdoor-indoor museum that gives credence to Bermuda's three centuries of seafaring history. The museum epitomizes the hardy spirit that kept the early colonists striving onward to keep their tiny island protected while using the sea as a constant source of commerce. One enters the museum area through an outer gate that was originally fronted by a moat and drawbridge. In the center of the Keepyard is a giant figure of Neptune, taken from a ship that saw her end near the close of the 19th century. The figurehead was first placed near Admiralty House at Spanish Point until it found a more living role in the new museum.

The main building, called the Queen's Exhibition Hall, was constructed of local stone by convicts in 1850 and has been beautifully restored and lit to show off a fine display of maritime maps, and salvaged artifacts from the *Sea Venture.* It is the type of museum that you can wander in at leisure. Of special delight is the Bermuda Fitted Dinghy exhibit in the eastern building, which features the 17-foot *Spirit of Bermuda* built in 1935 by two local men to sail to New York. This is housed in the two-storey Boat Loft, where there are many other tributes to the Bermudians who worked at shipbuilding during the last century. The small craft restoration workshop on the ground floor has a 14-foot fishing and mussel dinghy built more than 60 years ago and only discovered recently in rotting condition. There are plans to restore the boat, sail her, and make her a living exhibit. Also in the Boat Loft are a 13-foot turtle dinghy named *Magic,* in use from 1930 to 1973 (when the government banned turtle fishing), a 37-foot pilot gig (*Rambler*) considered to be the last locally built boat of its type, and the 14-foot *Victory.* This cedar vessel, built in 1885, had a fine racing reputation.

One can also wander among the gun emplacements and magazines for spectacular views of Grassy Bay and the Great Sound. See also the Treasure House, the History of Whaling, and the Turtle Fishing exhibitions. The museum is not yet finished. There are plans to refurbish the Commissioner's House up on the hill, which was built between 1823 and 1828 and is considered to be the most expensive residence ever constructed on a military base. The colonial-style building has stabling for 11 horses on the ground floor and ornate, grandiose moldings and plastering throughout. It is a fine example of cast-iron architecture and is a contrast to the simple and functional design that Bermudians developed for their own homes. Don't miss the Bermuda Arts Centre, across the street from the Commissioner's House, with its fine collection and changing exhibitions of many talented local artisans.

It is possible to catch the return ferry to Hamilton from the Freeport dock, very near the museum and dockyard.

Alternatively, one can cycle or bus back to Somerset and pick up the floral-laden route along East Shore Road, visiting the Gladys Morrell Nature Reserve near Cavello Bay. This two-acre space was presented to the National Trust in 1973 by the Sandys chapter of the Daughters of the Empire in memory of Mrs. Morrell.

The path is lined with hibiscus from about South View Road all the way to the end of the island. Just before the bridge on the east side is Lantana, a traditional and very attractive cottage colony. Try lunch at La Plage restaurant. The cycle path continues after the bridge, all the way to George's Bay Road, just before the boundary of Southampton Parish. Shortly thereafter, one can pick up Middle Road for the return journey to Warwick, Paget, and the rest of the island.

Southampton Parish

Southampton Parish presents a long, lean portrait from its boundary at Riddell's Bay to Tucker's Island, where the U.S. Naval Air Station Annex is now situated. Named after the third Earl of Southampton, this area, which has also been called Port Royal, offers a feeling of wide open spaces as well as breathtaking views of both the north and south shores.

Southampton's south shore from Stonehole Bay to Church Bay is spectacular and the public beach along Horseshoe Bay is one of the most photographed in the world. Not far out is a six-mile stretch of reef known as "The Boilers," because the constantly breaking surf along its top causes a boiling-like foam. The long continuous beaches along this coastline are only broken by cozy bays with craggy rocks and hardy shrubs that complement the clear blue waters. No photograph can do this area justice, for not only does the sea constantly change but the hues and subtleties of the sparkling sands move back and forth according to their moods. There is a complete metamorphosis from the bold and brilliant stance at high noon to the soft and delicate feeling that emerges at sunset.

The reverie is broken slightly at the Southampton Princess, high up on the hill and spilling all the way down to the sea. Located on 60 spectacular acres, the hotel is a younger sister to the Princess in Hamilton and was once partly owned by D. K. Ludwig, the famed American entrepreneuer. One story that goes around concerning the building of the new hotel is that Mr. Ludwig thought the prices quoted on the carpets (to be made in Taiwan) were too high, so he bought the carpet company.

This hotel is just like an American hotel, with its ultra-modern and luxurious accommodations, suites that have plush accoutrements and marble baths, and dark, air-conditioned lobby and shopping areas. On its property along the south shore, the hotel has opened a beach and tennis club and the Whaler Inn restaurant, which is hectic during the daytime but more civilized in the evening, when there is dancing on the terrace. Down on the other shore is the Waterlot Inn, which also belongs to the Southampton Princess. Now an expensive—but definitely not gourmet—place to dine, with waiters who don't seem to care, the restaurant is on the same site where an inn has been open, more or less, for the past 300 years. In the past, this has been a popular spot for Bermudians because they can come for a drink as easily by boat as by car (Bermudians are far more fond of their boats than they are of their automobiles).

In between the two shores are an 18-hole golf course, two swimming pools, shops, restaurants, nightspots, and guest rooms for 1,500 people, as well as facilities for conventions, seminars, and small group meetings.

Next to the Southampton Princess is Gibbs Hill and its famous lighthouse. When it was built between 1845 and 1846, it was the second iron lighthouse in the world. The project had first been discussed in 1830 but nothing was done until the next decade, when a survey proved that a total of 39 shipwrecks had occurred off the western end of the islands during this period, on reefs that extend as far as 16 miles off the shore.

Gibbs Hill stands 245 feet high and the lighthouse, which was constructed in England and brought over in pieces by ship, is 117 feet from base to light. The beam runs 362 feet above sea level and can be seen approximately 40 miles away by ships and 120 miles away by airplanes flying at 10,000 feet. Electricity finally replaced the original burner of four circular wicks in 1952, and light is now supplied by a 1,500-watt bulb located in the center of the lens. The lens makes a complete revolution every 50 seconds. It weighs two and three-quarter tons and contains 1,200 pounds of mercury. The machinery was formerly wound by hand every 30 minutes, but the winding mechanism was replaced by electrical equipment in 1964 and the entire operation is now automatic.

It is an easy climb of 185 steps to visit the top of the lighthouse. Not only can one see the highly polished brass gears of the light, but a small walkway around the top of the structure offers stupendous views of the entire Bermuda islands chain. The west end of the colony lies below, while the Great Sound and Hamilton lie beyond and just a little farther on is the unbroken expanse of open ocean.

Continuing along the South Shore Road, we come to Sonesta Beach Hotel nestled between Sinky Bay and Boat Bay. The Sonesta is another of the large and luxurious resort hotels and was designed to take full advantage of its site along the water. On the eastern side of the hotel is a pleasant cove where small craft are moored and fishermen come early in the morning to make their plans for the day. On the western side of the hotel is a charming, sandy beach in another cove where you can swim all year and learn the rudiments of scuba-diving before going onward to dive for sunken treasures.

At the top of the hill, overlooking Sonesta Beach, is the Henry VIII Restaurant and Pub. During the warm weather, the doors and windows are open and you can sit out on the stone terrace, overlooking the south shore. Farther along the coastline is The Reefs and its famed, beautiful beach, plus Christian Bay and Church Bay. At the end of the parish are West Whale Bay and Whitney Bay beaches, as well as the government-owned Port Royal Golf Course, an 18-hole championship course designed by Robert Trent Jones. This course is open to the public and players give it high marks for being a challenging and exciting game. A pro shop, restaurant, and tennis courts are all attached.

This end of Southampton was actually considered "overplus" land when the original survey was made by Richard Norwood in 1616. This consisted of some 200 acres that the governor, Daniel Tucker, took as his own and on which he proceeded to build himself a nice house. Naturally, this did not sit well with the shareholders of the Bermuda Company, so Governor Tucker was reconciled to having only a portion of this choice spot. However, the Tucker family went on to become one of the most prominent in Bermuda.

Colonel Henry Tucker and his family lived at The Grove in Southampton Parish. (Some feel that they built a stone house at the same site on which their ancestor Daniel had built a wooden mansion.) Colonel Henry is best known by us for his role in the theft of 100 kegs of gunpowder one August night in 1775 to help the American colonists in their "disagreement" with the Mother Country. He is also the father of Henry Tucker, whose house on Water Street in St. George belongs to the National Trust and is brimming with fine mementoes of the Tucker family and its accomplishments. Colonel Henry had six children, two of whom went to America to begin other branches of this fascinating family.

The little bay just before the boundary of the parish is called George's Bay (after Colonel Henry's son) and the island on which the U.S. Naval Air Station Annex is located was previously known as Tucker's Island.

Warwick Parish

Named after the second Earl of Warwick, another major shareholder in the Bermuda Company of 1610, this parish boasts a number of hotels and restaurants, two beautiful golf courses, lovely stretches of beach, and the oldest church of Scotland outside the mother country. The parish begins just past the Inverurie Hotel on the Harbour Road and near Surfside on the South Shore Road.

The Harbour Road boundary falls in line with Darrell's Wharf, a busy landing for the Hamilton ferry. Just opposite the dock is a beautiful old Bermudian home, one of several dotting this area. These large and elegant structures were obviously built more than a century ago, when the road was less wide and less traveled. As you pass by, notice the fine features of the traditional island roofs, doors, and windows, as well as the pastel exteriors. Occasionally, you can spot a water storage tank with its white-washed top or a separate buttery, both of which indicate an age gone by (modern storage tanks are built underground and refrigerators have re-placed butteries).

On the harbor side of the road are some small boat-building yards and off to the west is the bird-shaped Darrell's Island. The Darrell name is another Bermudian tradition and the family is widespread throughout the colony. A menu at the Waterlot Inn farther down the road (in Southampton) commemorates Claudia Darrell, who ran the place during the first part of this century. Claudia might be called the island's first feminist, for she apparently defied custom and took on male tasks. Many articles were written about Claudia, and her personality and energy are still very much a part of the island. Darrell's Island is also remembered because it's the site of Bermuda's first airport. The seaplanes that brought visitors from New York in the early 1930s landed here.

But, returning to our slow progression down the Harbour Road, we come to the Belmont dock and above, the Belmont Hotel and Golf Club. Sitting on 110 acres, the large pink structure belongs to the Trusthouse Forte family, together with the Harmony Club in Paget. The Belmont is known for its lovely views overlooking the Great Sound and for its 18-hole golf course that meanders around the hill and then extends over to the far side of Middle Road. Both the golf course and the tennis courts are open to nonmembers for a small fee. But reservations are necessary, so pay a visit to the pro shop, which is easily reached from the Harbour Road.

Continuing along Harbour Road, we turn to Burnt House Road (a name probably derivative of the 17th century when the only way to get rid of the devastating rats was to burn houses down), turning right on Middle Road and then right on Riddell's Bay Road just before the disco-theque/bar called Flavors. At the very end of the road is the Riddell's Bay Golf and Country Club, an 18-hole private course where the introduc-tion of a member or hotel is required for visitors to be able to play. Rid-dell's Bay was a haven for trading ships centuries ago and was originally called White Heron Bay, but the name was changed to honor a local family.

For a look at the South Shore side of Warwick Parish, we take Horse-shoe Road down to the South Road and travel east, coming first to War-wick Camp. These impressive blue-and-red-signed barracks were home for British troops during two world wars and now house the volunteer Bermu-da Regiment. There is an artillery range on the property, so do not be alarmed at the sound of shooting in the distance.

Jobson's Cove and Warwick Long Bay offer a magnificent stretch of public beaches along the south shore, with glorious cliffs and rocks and sand. One can spend the whole day here and never see it fully. This area is popular for picnics and body surfing and there are some interesting horse trails set far back from the swimming area. Motorbikes must be parked above in allotted spaces and are not allowed down on the shore. The whole area is beautifully kept and impressive at all times of the day and evening, any time of the year. A public camping area is also along this stretch of the shore.

There are a number of small housekeeping units here, which are worth a visit. The Mermaid Beach Club has a fine restaurant overlooking the water. Some scenes from *The Deep* were filmed at nearby Marley Beach.

Equestrians will want to visit the Spicelands Riding Centre and Tack Shop, which offers guided tours of Bermuda by horseback. Private or group lessons can be arranged for novices and the more advanced can take a breakfast ride along trails overlooking the pink South Shore beaches, followed by a large English breakfast served in an old Bermuda house. Bermudians are horsey people, in the tradition of their English forebears, and the Bermuda Hunt Club is small but active. The tack shop at the Spicelands Riding Centre sells caps and other paraphernalia at well below U.S. prices.

Other roads to be explored in Warwick are Spice Hill Road, Tamarind Vale, Cedar Hill and St. Mary's Road, Cobbs Hill Road, and Keith Hall Road, as well as the many Tribe Roads that cut across the parish from north to south. Wandering along these byways on your motorbike, drinking in the morning glory and oleander that line the edges, and enjoying the traditional houses that have been homes to generations of islanders is what Bermuda is all about.

Paget Parish

Paget is a parish you cannot miss. It begins at the edge of Hamilton Harbour and winds around Berry Hill Road on the east, faces the city of Hamilton on the north, and includes some of the colony's most beautiful and popular beaches along its south shore. Named after the fourth Lord Paget, the parish has a high concentration of residences because of its proximity to Hamilton, and many of its historic homes can be viewed, at least from the outside, by visitors. There are no golf courses in the parish and few open spaces other than the 36-acre Botanical Gardens estate and Paget Marsh.

Leaving Hamilton via Crow Lane, one can reach the Botanical Gardens via Berry Hill Road, Point Finger Road, or the South Shore Road. The Botanical Gardens are one of the colony's prime attractions and have steadily increased in size since 1898, when the Department of Agriculture took over the property. The gardens are still maintained by the Bermuda government and are open daily from sunrise to sunset. Conducted tours are offered on Tuesdays, Wednesdays, and Fridays from 10:30 A.M. and last approximately 90 minutes.

Throughout the year, the gardens are the site of various exhibitions and shows. These include an agricultural exhibition in April; dog shows in November and March; poultry, citrus, and bird shows; and periodic horse shows. Of the many permanent attractions, there is a garden for the blind, hibiscus garden, palm garden, cacti and succulent garden, orchid garden, aviary, and other exotic plant houses. In the center of the property is Camden House, a former private residence from one of the finest estates in Bermuda. The land, which once contained an arrowroot factory, now belongs to the gardens and the house is the official residence of Bermuda's premier.

It is open to the public on Tuesday and Friday afternoons from 12 noon to 2 P.M. Nearby is Tavern on the Green, where lunch and dinner are available (as well as alcoholic beverages). Local buses stop at the west and south gates and cycles can be parked on the grounds, near where the guided tours begin.

Driving west on Middle Road, we detour down to Hungry Bay, which is a popular spot for both fishermen and naturalists and where one can almost hear the sea roar like a hungry animal before an approaching storm. Nearby is Grape Bay, with its lovely beach, small hotel, and housekeeping cottages. Returning to Middle Road, we come to Rural Hill, where there are fine private residences such as Chelston, the official residence of the U.S. Consul General. This home, which is often on the spring Garden Club tour, sits high up on 14 acres of beautiful countryside. The house was acquired from the estate of an American businessman in 1954 and is perfect for entertaining. The property extends down to the south shore and the sea is accessible by walking through an old moon gate.

Another attractive home in the Rural Hill area is Inwood, just across Middle Road, set back a bit on the north side. Part of the house was built in 1650, but additions were made in 1700 by Colonel Francis Jones, a member of King William III's council in Bermuda. With these 18th-century additions, the structure is in the form of a cross, typical of the era. Inwood is also featured on the Garden Tour and is noted for its 12 powder rooms (where ladies and gentlemen of the day used to powder their wigs before joining the social gathering). The old cedar-beam ceilings are also an eye-catching feature.

To sidetrack a bit, take the Stowe Hill Road to Rosecote, the home and studio of Alfred Birdsey, unofficial artist laureate of Bermuda. Here one can chat with the artist or his family while rummaging about the small studio to look at the delightful watercolors, reproductions, and perhaps a commissioned oil painting. While Alfred Birdsey is known for his oil paintings, prints, and sketches of Bermuda's land and ocean scenes, his early cubist prints and, more recently, birds-on-the-wing moments, just might be the best Bermuda buy around. It is possible to visit Mr. Birdsey or his artist-daughters when they are in residence, if the visitor telephones ahead for an appointment. (See *Galleries and Artists* section for details.)

Continuing along Middle Road once again, one comes to Paget Marsh, a 26-acre area considered to be a gem among nature reserves. Owned by both the National Trust and the Audubon Society, the marsh contains some of the finest palmetto and cedar trees on the island as well as a mangrove swamp. This is the last place on the island where a forest remains intact as it appeared when the colonists first arrived. And, because this is the only safe refuge for some of the colony's endangered trees and plants, access is limited and visitors are requested to call the Trust office (292–6483) for permission to visit the area.

Nearby the marsh is St. Paul's, the parish church, which dates from 1796 and is considered young by Bermudian standards. At this juncture, one can pick up the South Shore Road for visits to Elbow Beach, Coral Beach, and Horizons and Cottages. This is one of the poshest parts of the south shore, of which Elbow Beach is the longest and most popular strand. The Elbow Beach Hotel began as a small guest house in 1908, then called the South Shore Hotel. Subsequently many additions were made and it is now among the largest of the resort hotels. Although the beach area is private, visitors are welcome for the day for a fee. During College Weeks, many of the springtime activities take place here.

The middle portion of the beach is public and the western end belongs to the Coral Beach Club, which used to be nothing more than a pleasant little restaurant and bathing facility but has become a fine tennis club. It is a private facility and you must have the introduction of a member to play. However, guests at the pleasant Horizons and Cottages have the use of this beautiful beach.

The harbor-side of Paget is equally beautiful and interesting. Leaving the city of Hamilton, one takes Crow Lane around to Waterville, the headquarters of the National Trust. Dating from the early part of the 18th century, the house originally belonged to the Triminghams, a merchant family who ran their business from here. On Harbour Road facing Pomander Walk is Red Hole, which was once a shipbuilding and repair center; now small craft are anchored here as well as carefully constructed.

Continuing along the Harbour Road, which is lined with morning glory, we pass by Clermont just before the Lower Ferry Landing. Clermont is a classic example of Bermuda Georgian architecture. It was built in 1800 by Thomas Butterfield, who was then chief justice of Bermuda. The house is well-known because another chief justice, Sir Brownlow Gray, built the island's first tennis court here in 1873 (the entire Gray family were early tennis enthusiasts). From this court, tennis was introduced to the United States via Mary Outerbridge, who took her equipment and a book of rules to the Staten Island Cricket Club. That was in 1874—look what has happened since!

The Hamilton ferry plies along this area in its quiet but efficient way. At the Hodsdon's Ferry Landing is the lovely guest house Newstead, with its fine view of the capital. The Salt Kettle dock is just a short walk to Glencoe, Greenbank, and Salt Kettle. Glencoe, the largest of the guest facilities, was a residence when President Woodrow Wilson made many visits here and stayed in what is now Room No. 7. Glencoe looks out on its own private harbor, where sunfish and dinghies are anchored, ready to set sail.

Farther down Harbour Road is Inverurie, a hotel that began its career in 1910 and has grown sideways and upwards since. The hotel is located just before the boundary to Warwick Parish and the Darrell's Wharf landing.

Taking Cobb's Hill Road straight across the island, you run into Middle Road and the Fourways Inn, one of the colony's best and most prestigious restaurants. Here one can dine in an old-world atmosphere, in a former Georgian-style home that was built of coral and Bermuda cedar around 1727. When the weather is friendly, the delightful courtyard becomes another dining room. French cuisine and Bermudian specialties are served.

The Fourways Inn and Cottage Colony is open daily for brunch, lunch, and dinner (gourmet brunch on Sundays and Thursdays). Reservations are a must because both the food and the ambiance are as popular with Bermudians as they are with visitors.

Pembroke Parish

If you are sailing into Hamilton Harbour aboard a large cruise ship, grab a spot on the top deck to watch the many islands and water traffic

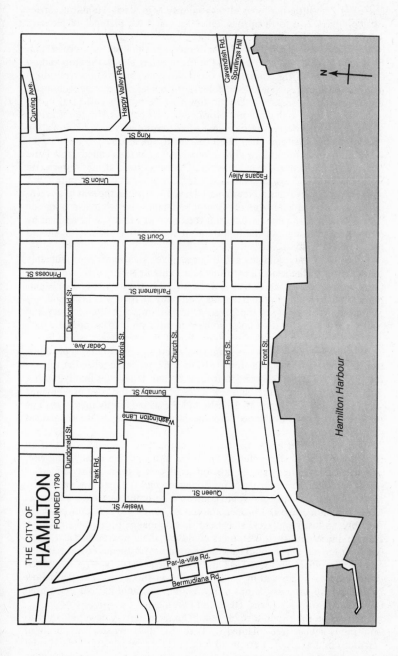

THE CITY OF
HAMILTON
FOUNDED 1790

glide by. The little harbor is always full of cargo ships, Hamilton ferries that ply back and forth in their quiet way, and the plethora of pleasure craft that give Bermuda its nickname, "Land of Water."

The first view of the city of Hamilton from the deck of a cruise ship is always a thrill because one sees the Front Street shops, the stop-and-go traffic in front of the "birdcage" (does the policeman inside really help the flow or does he just add local color?), the horses and carriages clumped under the shady trees, the Gothic tower of Bermuda's cathedral up on the hill, and the Italianate pink towers of the Sessions House off to the right. The thrill evolves into a sense of adventure as you walk down the steps into the Customs shed and cross on to the street.

Hamilton was founded in 1790, around what was then called Crow Lane Harbour, for the purpose of collecting Customs duties at the western end of the island. The town was named after Governor Henry Hamilton, but was a slow achiever until New Year's Day, 1815, when the seat of government was moved here from St. George's. There were two reasons for the move: One was the fine harbor, and the other was that residences had by now spread throughout the island and it was felt that the capital should be more centrally located.

Hamilton today comprises 150 acres, gives shelter to approximately one-quarter of the island's entire population, and is Bermuda's only city. It is part of Pembroke Parish, named after the third Earl of Pembroke, a major shareholder in the Bermuda Company in 1616 when the land was surveyed. While most of the government buildings are 19th century and fairly staid, the city does boast some romantic landmarks, one of which is the charming, white-washed Perot Post Office on Queen Street.

William Bennett Perot was Hamilton's first and most famous postmaster, serving in the position from 1816 to 1862, when he retired at the age of 72. Perot's father, descended from a French Huguenot family, built a large, rambling structure on a few acres of land at the edge of what was then the center of Hamilton in 1814 and the whole family moved in. The excess acreage was developed into fine gardens and the estate was named Par-la-Ville.

Perot shared an annex of the main house with a friend who had an apothecary and, as he preferred puttering in his garden to anything else, his friend Heyl often ran the post office. It cost a penny to send a letter from Hamilton to St. George's (or Somerset) and the mail was carried by boat. But, alas, customers would come in after hours to leave mail for delivery but not leave the proper amount of pennies. This annoyed Perot terribly, so his friend Heyl suggested that he make "postage stamps" for sale in sheets and then customers could cut them apart and paste them on their letters. Perot could cancel the stamp when the letter was received in the post office. This was 1848 and the famous Perot postage stamp was born; today it is coveted by collectors all over the world. The Perot Post Office, where you buy stamps today, is the very building that Perot used and shared with his friend Heyl, the pharmacist.

Next door, in the comfortable family home with its wide verandahs and enormous rubber tree (planted by Perot in 1847), where Perot brought up nine children, is the Bermuda Library, Historical Society, and Colonial Archives. The lovely gardens that Perot nurtured along and enjoyed so much are now a public park. On view in the house are a map of Bermuda believed to be drawn by Sir George Somers around 1610; his sea chest, and portraits of him and Lady Somers painted during their lifetimes. Also on view are the models of the *Sea Venture, Deliverance,* and *Patience,* three ships that played an important role in the colonization of Bermuda, lovely antique cedar furniture and silver made by the early settlers, a copy of the first surveyor's map of 1616, and a sedan chair used in St. George's in the 18th century. Other objects of interest to visitors are some oil coinage (hog money, it was called), a model of the famous Bermuda dinghy, and a copy of the letter that George Washington sent from his camp in Cambridge, Massachusetts, to the citizens of Bermuda in September 1775 to beg for the gunpowder stored on the island (before the general knew that it had already been "lifted" onto two American warships and was in possession of the Continental Congress). Mementoes of the American Civil War and the 350th anniversary celebration of the Bermuda colony are also in evidence. The museum is small enough so you can take in all the displays without getting tired. Take a walk in Par-la-Ville gardens afterward and think of the eccentric postmaster who created a stamp to keep his customers honest.

Walking up Queen Street and turning right on Church Street, you come upon Hamilton's City Hall on the left, a handsome modern building with a traditional Bermudian feeling and a weathervane in the shape of the *Sea Venture.* City Hall is more than just an administrative building—it is the center of the island's cultural activities. It has a fine theater where musical and dramatic performances are held and films are shown. The upstairs hall is utilized for exhibitions and trade shows and for the display of local crafts throughout the year. The building also houses an art gallery that has a revolving exhibit of local and foreign works. The cedar balustrade and large doors to the public rooms are well worth a visit. The building was designed by a local architect and contains a Time Capsule to be opened on the 500th anniversary of the colony, in the year 2109.

In the next block on Church Street is Bermuda's Cathedral of the Most Holy Trinity, dedicated in 1894 on the site of an earlier church that was destroyed by arson in 1844. (It was the building of this cathedral that stopped construction of the church in St. George's—now known as the Unfinished Cathedral.) The structure is built mainly from native limestone. Decorative touches are of marble, granite, and English oak, and stone from Caen (Normandy) has been used for the moldings of doorways and windows. It is a beautiful building that is tenderly cared for by its congregation. For commemorative Sundays, for example, the women of the church guild create beautiful floral arrangements. The kneeling cushions are all handmade. The stained-glass windows and small chapels add to a feeling of happiness, even on a dull day. The Warrior Chapel, dedicated in 1977, contains the flags of the armed forces connected with Bermuda, two throne chairs for use on royal occasions, and three kneeling desks for private prayer. High up on the east wall is the Angel Window, designed and donated by a local Bermudian artist. On the wall near the lectern is a copy of an eighth-century Canterbury Cross, given by the friends of Canterbury Cathedral and set in stones from that structure. The west doors are made from wood imported from British Guyana.

Turning down Parliament Street, one sees the main post office on the right (on the site of the famous old jail) and Sessions House on the left. In this building with its pink Italian towers, the House of Assembly meets upstairs under the portraits of King George III and Queen Charlotte, while the Bermuda Supreme Court has moved to Front Street. The Speaker of the House as well as the Chief Justice and barristers all wear the traditional English wig and black robes. There are galleries in the upper floors for visitors who may want to view a bit of "colonialism." The ornate additions to the outer face of the building were added after 1818 and the clock tower commemorates Queen Victoria's Jubilee year of 1887.

In front of Sessions House is the Cabinet Building. Built around 1840 of native limestone, it is this building in which the governor convenes Parliament at the end of October each year. He delivers an address to the legislature while standing in front of a "throne," an old Bermudian cedar chair on which is carved "Governor Josiah Forster, 1642." The Cenotaph Memorial in front of the building honors the colony's war dead, and the cornerstone was laid by the Prince of Wales in 1920 (who later became Edward VIII and abdicated to marry Mrs. Simpson). Bermudians love royalty and are always excited by visits of the royal family. Queen Elizabeth paid a visit during her coronation year and again during her Silver Jubilee. Prince Charles came to celebrate the 350th anniversary of Bermuda's Parliament in 1970 and read the "throne speech" in historic St. Peter's Church, where the first Parliament had convened in 1620. Princess Margaret arrived in 1984 and unveiled a statue of Sir George Somers on the 375th anniversary of his discovery of the islands.

Across Court Street is the former Town Hall, a small and compact building with beautiful cedar doors that now houses the Supreme Court. At this juncture Front Street becomes East Broadway. Turning left on King Street, you can walk or ride up to Happy Valley Road and then into Fort Hamilton for a spectacular panoramic view of the city and harbor.

During the mid-19th century, Bermuda's defenses were heavily built up following a plan devised by the Duke of Wellington, hero of the defeat of Napoleon at Waterloo. The Wellington plan was to transform Bermuda into the "Gibraltar of the West" and featured the building of more forts to protect the channels. Fort Hamilton was one of the 13 fortifications built during this period. They were never really needed and were outdated by the time they were completed. Closed for many years because of unsanitary conditions, Hamilton's Victorian fortification has been restored and is now considered a historic monument.

Visitors approach the main gate over a moat, now dry and filled with exotic plants that thrive in this protected and damp area. The moat can be reached from the underground galleries. On the upper level, now a grassy slope filled with park benches, the Royal Arms of Queen Victoria are emblazoned on the main armaments. Some Bermudians even feel that the fort is the embodiment of the old queen herself, frowning down upon the city of Hamilton and its harbor.

Returning to the center of town, we walk once again down Front Street past the busy piers to Albuoy's Point, named after a 17th-century doctor who fought one of the many fever epidemics on the island. Here, next to the modern Bank of Bermuda structure, is the Visitor's Service Bureau, the Chamber of Commerce, the dock for local ferries, and the Royal Bermuda Yacht Club. The club itself was conceived under the calabash tree in Walsingham (that Tom Moore made famous in his poetry) by a group of keen sailors in 1844. Within a year, the group had obtained permission from the throne to use the word "Royal" and received the patronage of the royal family. The members of the club have always encouraged international racing and sponsor the glamorous Newport to Bermuda race that draws together some of the world's best sailing yachts every other year. It begins in Newport, Rhode Island, and the finish line is at St. David's Head, the most eastern part of Bermuda. The yachts then sail into Hamilton Harbour and anchor off the yacht club for a few days before returning to their home port. The clubhouse, on the western side of Albuoy's Point, was built in the 1930s.

Farther down Pitt's Bay Road is the Princess Hotel in Hamilton, named in honor of Princess Louise, daughter of Queen Victoria, who came for a visit during the winter of 1883. This hotel has undergone a great many additions since it was completed. A year after it was built, the hotel was already too small to accommodate the number of visitors who wished to stay there.

During the early part of this century, the Princess was *the* hotel and one of the social centers of the colony for both visitors and residents attending tea dances and grand balls. Later, between the World Wars, the Princess had some competition from other new hotels going up, but she held her own and at the outbreak of World War II played her most important and exciting role. The place where the beautiful people had trod in fun and finery was now the headquarters of censorship throughout the British Empire. In the basement of the elegant Princess Hotel, experts read and analyzed mail from all over the world being carried to Europe via Pan Am flights, which were instructed to land in Bermuda between New York and Lisbon.

The Princess, which used to have spacious lawns and tennis courts, now has several additions to accommodate more people and recently underwent a $20 million renovation.

Around the corner from the Princess Hotel is Pitt's Bay, a nicely protected boat anchorage for small craft and the beginning of a residential section that extends all the way to the end of the peninsula of Pembroke Parish. One of these fine old private residences is Norwood, named after Richard Norwood, Bermuda's first surveyor, who acquired the property in 1657. The house was built in 1707 by his granddaughter. It is well known for the amusing sign at its gate: "Where tramps must not, Surely ladies and gentlemen will not trespass." The house, sometimes on the Houses and Gardens Tour (organized by the Garden Club) in the spring, was originally built in the shape of a cross to ward off evil spirits. There is also a maze of clipped bushes in the garden, fashioned after those in Hampton Court. It is still a unique feature of the spacious gardens. The house overlooks Pitt's Bay and Saltus Island, just before the two juts of land known as Point Shares and Mill Shares.

At the end of the peninsula belonging to Pembroke Parish is Spanish Point, a rather desolate rocky area where a group from the *Sea Venture* believed they found evidence that the Spaniards had camped here some years before. (It was probably Captain Diego Ramirez who wrote a description of the islands and drew a detailed map in 1603.) At the end of the point is Cobbler's Island, where executed slaves were exhibited as a warning for their colleagues.

Returning to Hamilton via Cox's Hill, you pass Admiralty House, which is no longer used and is now a park. It was built in the early 1800s but rebuilt many times, and one admiral known for his fondness of caves had several constructed underneath the grounds. Also on the grounds are several trees planted by visiting royalty in the late 19th and early 20th centuries. It was during this period that being a member of the Royal Navy was a prestigious position. But since the British forces were withdrawn from Bermuda in the late 1950s, there has been no need for an Admiralty House. It is only part of a glorious and glamorous past.

Grouped in an area just north of the city boundary are the Government Tennis Stadium, St. John's Church, Black Watch Well and Pass, and Government House. St. John's, the parish church of Pembroke, was built in 1625 and stands on the site of the first church in Pembroke. Originally known as Spanish Point Church, it has been enlarged many times and its historic yard is full of the tombs of men who guided the capital and the colony along. In fact, a graveyard was the scene of an unusual drama one afternoon in 1875 when two opposing ministers arrived to read a funeral speech and each tried to outdo the other by speaking louder. Later, the resident minister of St. John's brought a "trespass" suit against the other man (from another Protestant sect) and won his case. The judge fined the defendant the sum of one shilling.

From St. John's Church, climb the hill to Mount Langton and you'll come across Black Watch Well, which gets its name from the fact that a detachment of this famous regiment dug a well at the request of the governor during the great drought of 1849. Mount Langton is also the site of Government House, the official residence of the colony's governor. The land was purchased by the colony soon after the capital moved to Hamilton in 1815, but the original two-story structure that was on the grounds has given way to a much more impressive and imposing building. The lovely grounds are full of trees and bushes planted by important people, and it was here Governor Richard Sharples and his aide, Captain Hugh Sayers, were assassinated in the spring of 1973 by a local dissident.

Returning down Marsh Folly Road again, we come to the government tennis stadium where visitors may enjoy all the privileges of the tennis club and watch some fine local matches. Nearby, on Cedar Avenue, is Victoria Park, which was built to commemorate the Queen's Golden Jubilee in 1887. At lunchtime, the park is full of workers from the area.

Hamilton has the greatest concentration of restaurants on the island. You can get simple snacks from a pushcart near the park or local specialties of freshly caught seafood from the eating places along the harbor. Most visitors prefer to sit on the terraces of the many restaurants that line Front Street, watching the people pass by below. With the colorful backdrop of small craft in the water beyond, it is a delightful scene, especially on a sunny day.

It is best to plan one's day in Hamilton around shopping, sightseeing, and viewing the legislature (when in session). During the winter season or Rendezvous Time (mid-November to April), the Department of Tourism plans special events for visitors, such as a dine-around program, exhibitions of local crafts, noon performances of the skirling ceremony at Fort Hamilton, botanical garden tours, walking tours of St. George's, Fort St. Catherine, the sights of West End, the island of Somerset, and the Bermuda Arts Centre at the Dockyard. Golfers are welcome to take part in a tournament at the Port Royal Golf Course. The 16th-century ceremony of Beating Retreat can be viewed on Front Street and in St. George's, year-round. Performed by a volunteer corps of the Bermuda Regiment and Bermuda Cadet Pipe Band, the ceremony is traditionally performed at sunset, much as it was when the ancient towns of England were surrounded by fortifications and all were warned to return to the protection within before nightfall.

If you plan to spend the evening in Hamilton, most restaurants require advance reservations and the majority prefer that gentlemen wear a jacket and tie (see *Dining, Wining, and Entertainment* section). The action in local nightclubs begins around 10 P.M. and winds down in the wee hours of the morning. Taxis can always be found in the area. There is a surcharge after midnight.

Devonshire Parish

Wandering through Devonshire Parish is a bit like wandering around the back roads of the English countryside, for this area of Bermuda seems to be more lush, more green, and more hilly than the rest of the island. There are few commercial enterprises here, just a few housekeeping apartments and one cottage colony (along the south coast), no restaurants, and just one very large nightspot, the Clay House Inn, along the north coast. Named after the first Earl of Devonshire, the parish does boast a public golf course, marsh land, a nature reserve, some gardens, and a historic old church.

Old Devonshire Church stands smack in the middle of the parish on the Middle Road. Built plain and simple like an early Bermuda cottage, the foundation of this building was erected around 1716, although the first structure on this site dates from 1624. It is now known as Old Devonshire Church but was formerly called Christ Church. Unfortunately, what we visit today is a reconstruction. On Easter Sunday 1970, the old building was largely demolished by an explosive. Many beautiful and historic pieces were lost in the fire that resulted, including the font and organ, but some were saved and restored.

The building is constructed of local limestone and cedar, following the early shipwright technique. The vestry is to the north, the chancel to the east. An extension built in 1806 to house the organ loft is still evident in the west wing. All of the pews face the three-tiered pulpit and communion table, which are both believed to be from the original 17th-century church and fortunately were saved from the 1970 fire. Some pieces of church silver date from 1590 and are said to be the oldest on the island. A cedar chest, believed to have once held the church records, also appears to date from the early 17th century, for it was obviously built before the Bermuda Company forbade the use of timber cedar for the making of chests around 1650. Other pieces that have survived are an old cedar armchair, candelabra, a cross, and a cedar screen. Until the fire, there was no electricity in the church and evening services were by candlelight, but the structure is now wired for electricity. The building has a cool, puritan feeling and is a soothing place to visit on a warm day.

Nearby is Devonshire Marsh, or what the Bermudians refer to as a "brackish pond." In the early days, the entire parish was called Brackish Pond. Today there is a large distillation plant in the parish as well as subterranean wells that supply a great deal of fresh water to the island.

The north coast of Devonshire is craggy and lined with cliffs. Again one might think of England except for the beautiful turquoise sea that places Bermuda apart from almost anywhere else in the world. Close to the border of Pembroke is Devonshire Dock, where local fishermen come in the afternoon to measure their catch. This is a good place to buy dinner if you are staying in a housekeeping unit. If not, it's a good place to pick up some salty jargon.

Along the south coast of Devonshire is the lovely cottage colony called Ariel Sands, with its own private beach, as well as Devonshire Bay with its public beach area. Halfway between the two are geologic exposures that show three stages of development in the formation of the islands.

Along the South Shore Road are two other places of interest. The Edmund Gibbons Nature Reserve (just west of the junction with Collector's Hill) is marshland that provides living space for a number of birds and rare species of Bermuda flora. It is open daily. Visitors are advised not to enter the marshy area. Just west of Devonshire Bay Road is the Palm Grove Garden, set behind a beautiful old traditional home that faces the South Road. It is open daily (except Sunday) from 9 A.M. to 5 P.M. The private estate also has a fine collection of tropical birds.

The arboretum, along Corkscrew Hill Road, is another natural area that is worth a visit on a hot day. Take a stroll among the cool trees, especially fragrant after a brief rain.

Devonshire's public nine-hole golf course is called the Ocean View Golf and Country Club and is open to visitors for a green's fee. Stop by and pay a visit to the pro, Rogers Outerbridge, and make arrangements for a lesson or a game.

Other interesting areas to visit in Devonshire are Fort Hill and Montpelier Road, Orange Valley Road and Parsons Road, Jubilee, Brighton Hill, and Hermitage roads. The names alone are enough to entice anyone to take a little ride on a motorbike.

Smith's Parish

Bordering Harrington Sound on the east and the open sea on the north and south, Smith's Parish was named after Sir Thomas Smith, another prominent benefactor of the Bermuda Company. The parish encompasses Flatts Village, two lovely bird sanctuaries, a superbly restored 17th-century home, and Spanish Rock, which may or may not give a clue about early visitors to the island. Local historians cannot agree on the significance of this rock on which crude carvings were found.

During the 17th and 18th centuries, Flatts was a smuggler's haven and ships used to stop here in the dark of night to unload their goods before continuing on to the eagle eyes of the Customs officials at St. George's. Today this little village with old-world charm and lovely views of both the inlet and Harrington Sound is just a shadow of its former self, with a few small shops, cycle liveries, and a marine center. Don't miss the aquarium, which opened in 1928 in Flatts, 15 minutes from Hamilton. It now houses some 31 tanks and one giant reef tank and displays over 107 species of fish and 109 species of marine vertebrates in a natural setting. Nearby is the Palmetto Hotel and Cottages.

Taking Harrington Sound Road out of Flatts Village, there are breathtaking views of the sound along an oleander-lined byway. Just past the juncture of Knapton Hill Road, you come to Devil's Hole, which might be called Bermuda's first visitor attraction. Originally a fish pond, the owner (a Mr. Trott) decided to build a wall around it in 1830 and within a few years, he was charging an entrance fee. All types of fish and turtles swim peacefully together here in what was probably a cave. For a fee, you can tug on the baited but hookless line and have some fun. You can tell big fish stories back home because whatever you catch must go back. Free admission and open daily.

Winterhaven Farmhouse is just west of Devil's Hole. It is a Bermuda National Trust property and is open to the public Mondays and Thursdays, 2 P.M. to 5 P.M. Continuing on Harrington Sound Road, we come to the North Nature Reserve at the western end of Mangrove Lake and just inside the boundary of Smith's Parish. The reserve features living mangroves that attract several unique types of birds, as well as other water flora and fauna. The reserve is open daily and there is no admission fee.

Returning along the South Shore Road, you pass by Pink Beach Club and cottages, a deluxe cottage colony with its own private beach, John Smith's Bay, and the site of Spanish Rock. Located between Spittal Pond, the most spectacular of the nature reserves, and the shore, Spanish Rock has long been a riddle to Bermudians. A cryptic inscription was found by the early settlers, crudely carved on a high bluff overlooking the ocean. The original inscription had a "TF" and the date 1543 and was believed to be attributed to a Spanish explorer of the 16th century named Theodore Fernando Camelo. Others feel that Portuguese explorers may have been in the area during this period and left their mark. Local historians do not agree and it makes for a lively argument. However, the original Spanish Rock is no longer and what one sees is but a bronze cast.

The adjoining 60-acre Spittal Pond is a wildlife sanctuary preserved by both the National Trust and the Bermuda Audubon Society. It is a nature lover's paradise for long walks and observation. Between November and May, about 25 species of waterfowl come here to roost. Spittal Pond is open daily. Visitors are advised to keep to the pathways provided.

Continuing on the South Shore Road, turn right at Collector's Hill for Verdmont, a fine example of a 17th-century Bermuda mansion and the most important of the Trust properties. Now open as a museum, the house is practically unchanged since it was built sometime between 1616 and 1662 and is a lesson in exactly how these early buildings were designed. Although the house was lived in continuously until the 1950s, it never had inside plumbing or electricity.

Verdmont was most likely built by Captain William Sayle, who owned 50 acres of property that stretched from the north shore to the south shore and chose this hill as the site of his home. Sayle was three times governor of Bermuda; in between, he led expeditions to colonize the island of Eleuthera in the Bahamas as well as a part of South Carolina. He was as colorful a character as he was a staunch Cromwellian and died in 1671 while serving as the first governor of South Carolina.

The house eventually landed in the hands of Thomas Smith, a Customs collector, who sold his house in St. George to Henry Tucker (now the President Henry Tucker House) in 1775 when he moved to Verdmont. One of his daughters married John Green, who also became a Customs collector, as well as a highly regarded portrait artist. Some of Green's portraits, including a miniature self-portrait, are now hanging in the house. The home was subsequently inherited by minor relations (the Greens had no children) and the last person to live in Verdmont was an eccentric spinster who lived there for 75 years and refused to make any modern improvements, such as installing electricity or plumbing. When she died in 1953, Verdmont was purchased by the Bermuda Historical Monuments Trust (predecessor to the National Trust), renovated, and opened as a museum.

Entry to the house is now by the back door on the north side of the building, next to what is considered the handsomest early stairwell in Bermuda. The newel posts on each landing were designed with removable caps so that candles could be placed at strategic intervals in the evening. Early staircases were, of course, made of local cedar by hand and they became much-admired showpieces.

The house is large and square, with double chimneys on either side to provide a fireplace in every room. This was strictly for comfort, as cooking and other necessities were handled outside in an attached building. Each room also has three large windows with splendid views of both shores, and some still have the old, iridescent glass. The window shutters are on the inside, in Williamsburg fashion, and not in the typical island tradition of "push out" blinds that were copied from the Caribbean. The absence of shutters or blinds on the outside does give the building a rather naked look and causes one to wonder how the old glass could have withstood storms all these centuries.

The house is furnished in English and Bermudian antiques, most of which have been lent by local residents. The downstairs rooms include a library, parlor, drawing room, and dining room. Upstairs are four identical rooms now furnished as a bedroom, nursery, upstairs parlor, and Oriental room. One cannot be quite sure that the avid interest much of the Western world had in the Orient in the 18th century was shared by the colonists, but nevertheless, enough antiques of the period were found on the island to warrant such a room. In what is now furnished as an upstairs parlor (but was undoubtedly a proper bedroom) is a china coffee service reputed to be a gift from Napoleon to George Washington. But the American statesman never received his gift because the ship bringing it across the Atlantic was seized and brought to Bermuda. Its cargo was condemned as contraband under the order of John Green (who owned Verdmont). It was sold at auction and the coffee service was purchased by a Bermudian whose descendants eventually donated it to the Verdmont museum.

There is a lovely little balcony off the second floor from which to view the south shore. The open-well staircase continues on to the attic, which covers almost the entire floor plan and has a headroom of over seven feet. Some feel that the top-floor staircase was added a century after the house was built and that the attic was developed to expand the family quarters. Or, did some secret privateering go on here? Verdmont has many secrets. Without a doubt this is one of the island's most intriguing spots to visit.

Hamilton Parish

This parish offers a number of sightseeing attractions, as well as a diversity in scenery and natural phenomena. Named after the second Marquis of Hamilton, the parish winds around three-quarters of Harrington Sound, which is actually a saltwater lake some six miles long. The parish also borders the Atlantic Ocean on the north and south and Castle Harbour on the east. The southern section of the parish, tucked between Smith's and St. George's, houses half of the Mid-Ocean Golf Course as well as two other brackish ponds, Mangrove Lake and Trotts Pond, which boast a full complement of fascinating water flora and fauna.

The western boundary of Hamilton Parish is Flatts Inlet, where Bermuda's aquarium has resided since 1928, with a collection of sea life that ranks high in the world. Noted as the island's top tourist attraction, the aquarium has 32 tanks ranging in size from five gallons for a sea horse family to 40 feet for the long reef tank. On display at one time are about 107 species of fish and 109 species of marine vertebrates that inhabit the seas around Bermuda. All the fish are caught locally and the tanks are supplied with fresh water from Harrington Sound.

The aquarium also houses tortoises from the Galapagos, an open aviary for tropical birds, flamingoes, and lots of monkeys. There are also two harbor seals from Labrador. Connected to the aquarium is a natural history museum that houses specimens of Bermuda's game fish, rare seashells, artifacts recovered from sunken ships, and local crafts of Bermuda cedar. The adjacent children's zoo, consisting primarily of small farm animals, is open in the summertime only.

Following the North Shore Road around to Bailey's Bay, we pass a long stretch known as Shelly Bay, which was a major shipbuilding area from the 17th to 19th centuries. The bay was named for one of the passengers aboard the *Sea Venture,* who discovered it while exploring this end of the island. Crawl Hill, just before Bailey's Bay, is the highest point in the parish and offers superb views of the north shore. Digress a minute and turn down Trinity Church Road to Church Bay on Harrington Sound. Here amid a peaceful setting is the Hamilton Parish Church, originally built with just one long room in 1623. Over 350 years of reconstruction and loving care have made this into one of the most delightful churches in the entire colony and certainly worth a detour.

Returning to the North Shore Road, we come to Bailey's Bay, also named for a 17th-century citizen, which now encompasses the whole northeastern part of the parish. Continuing on the North Shore Road you'll come to the Bermuda Perfumery, established in 1931 and a successful enterprise ever since. Free guided tours are offered daily. The tour guide explains the process of cultivating the flowers (lily and passion flowers are the favorites), extracting the scent, preserving it, and combining it with alcohol to make the perfume. These fragrances are noted for their sweetness and are made for both men and women. They can be bought at the factory and shipped worldwide for a nominal fee. On the lovely grounds of the perfume factory is a quaint gift shop housed in what looks like a miniature English cottage.

Another interesting "factory" to visit is a short step away on Blue Hole Hill. Bermuda pottery is made and sold here in a studio/workshop atmosphere. Visitors are welcome to view the creation of locally made pottery. Blue Hole Hill is also the home of the Blue Grotto Dolphin Show, where the famous fish perform all their tricks and acrobatics in a lovely setting. Every day is the day of the dolphins and there are five shows between 11 A.M. and 4 P.M. (Admission is $3 for adults, $1.25 for children under 12.)

The whole area between Bailey's Bay and Castle Harbour is full of caves, most of which were only discovered in this century. They have such colorful names as Admiral's Cave, Prospero's, Cathedral, Church, Crystal, and Leamington. Both Leamington and Crystal caves are open to the public and have been equipped with wooden footbridges that cross the clear, subterranean lakes, as well as floodlights that make the stalactites and stalagmites even more translucent and dramatic.

Crystal Cave was discovered in 1907 when two young boys were playing ball and the ball disappeared into a hole in the ground. When they burrowed after it, they found themselves in a vast cavern surrounded by fantastic shapes of stalag formations. The cave they found is 120 feet below the surface, now reached by a wet, sloping walkway. A guide explains the formations and then works wonders with the lighting system to make such dramatic silhouettes as the New York skyline and Disneyland characters. If you like to go underground, you should not miss either of these commercial enterprises.

Grotto Bay Beach and Tennis Club has two caves on its property. One is called Cathedral Cave and can only be explored on hands and knees. The other, formerly a discotheque, is now a "romantic lounge" featuring music from the 1930s to the 1960s. (Some say that Shakespeare took refuge here and wrote *The Tempest,* but don't believe a word of it.)

There are two popular dining spots in Bailey's Bay. The Swizzle Inn is a favorite rest stop for cyclists and bills itself as the home of the rum swizzle, which might be called Bermuda's national drink. Here one can sit on the small terrace and watch the traffic while enjoying a refreshing rum swizzle and a swizzleburger, another house specialty. In the evening, the inn is full of locals who stop by for a chat with friends and a good game of darts and, of course, a swizzle or two.

Next to the Leamington Cave is a small branch of Trimingham's as well as the Plantation Restaurant, which features Bermudian food in a casual atmosphere. This restaurant is one of the few places on the island that offers a table d'hôte menu and is well worth a visit.

Continuing along Harrington Sound Road with its peaceful scenery, you'll see a sign that says "Tom Moore's Tavern." Follow the arrow down a long path to Walsingham Bay. This is the home with its calabash tree that was immortalized by the Irish poet Tom Moore during his four-month visit to the colony in 1804. The bay is named after one of the castaways on the *Sea Venture,* and when Samuel Trott, a local magistrate, bought the property in the 17th century and built a family home, it was naturally named Walsingham.

The home remained in the Trott family for several generations. Tom Moore came here to visit a descendant (also named Samuel Trott) and his daughters and to sit under the calabash tree in the front yard where he composed romantic verse. It is this same tree that a group of gentlemen sailors sat under in 1844 to form the Royal Bermuda Yacht Club. The house was turned into a tavern about 75 years ago, was closed in 1980, and has recently reopened. The woods that surround the old house are much the same as they were three centuries ago, and it is pleasant to sit on the dock overlooking Walsingham Bay. In the evening, the house and grounds are especially romantic and you too feel compelled to write your own love poetry while partaking of local seafood.

Overlooking Castle Harbour, on an impressive 260-acre piece of property, is one of the colony's largest and most elegant resort hotels. Commissioned by the Furness-Withy Steamship Line in 1929, the Castle Harbour hotel opened in 1931, complete with an 18-hole golf course. It is a splendid property, adjacent to the famous Mid-Ocean Club, which the steamship line developed a decade earlier. During World War II, the hotel was occupied by the U.S. forces, but it has been restored several times in the ensuing four decades. Now operated by the Marriott Corporation, the Castle Harbour Resort is in full swing following its latest multimillion-dollar renovation.

Continuing on Harrington Sound Road, one jogs slightly into Tucker's Town proper and St. George's Parish and then again into the southern extension of Hamilton Parish. The hibiscus-lined road continues all the way around the sound and back up to Flatts Village. Alternatively, you can turn left on Paynters Road for a ride through the golf course and then along the south shore, passing Trotts Pond and Mangrove Lake. The views are splendid on both routes.

St. George's Parish

St. George's Parish is often called the genesis of Bermuda, because it is here at the eastern end of the islands where colonization all began. Off what is now called St. Catherine's Point, the *Sea Venture* was wrecked in 1609. The *Sea Venture* was one of seven vessels that sailed from Plymouth, England, in May of that year to carry provisions and colonists to the new and struggling settlement on the James River (Virginia). About a week from the coast of the New World, the *Sea Venture* encountered a severe storm and was blown off course. Land was sighted after some bad days in the rolling sea, but before the little vessel could make her way into a harbor, she was thrown upon a reef and totally wrecked. Under the careful guidance of Sir George Somers, admiral of the fleet, and Sir Thomas Gates, who later became governor of Jamestown, all 150 passengers on board landed safely and took up residence for almost a year on St. George's Island.

The castaways built two new ships, the *Deliverance* and the *Patience*, and sailed away in the spring of 1610 for Jamestown. But they knew they had found a beautiful spot in the Atlantic Ocean and two years later, the same company that founded Jamestown sent fifty-odd adventurous folk to settle this lovely isle. They arrived in 1612 aboard the *Plough* and (after a brief stop on Smith's Island) founded the town of St. George, named after Sir George Somers and St. George, the patron saint of England. Walking through this delightful town, which has not changed much since the 17th century, one cannot help but feel a sense of history and the footsteps of these early settlers on the well-worn paths. This remained the capital of Bermuda for 203 years, until a move to Hamilton in 1815 was precipitated by the fact that the harbor was better for trading ships and that the island's capital should be placed at the center of its inhabitants.

King's Square is the heart of St. George, with its cedar replicas of Stocks and Pillory, Town Hall, Visitors' Service Bureau, and bridge leading to Ordnance Island. Off the square to the west is Water Street, where you'll find the post office, President Henry Tucker's home, and Somers Wharf.

The cedar replicas of Stocks and Pillory are a source of fun for all ages and no one should miss the opportunity to be photographed in them. The original models stood on this site some 300 years ago and, according to legend, were in good use. Another form of punishment in the 17th century was the Ducking Stool, which can be seen on Ordnance Island. One wonders which would be worse, being dunked in the cold sea several times

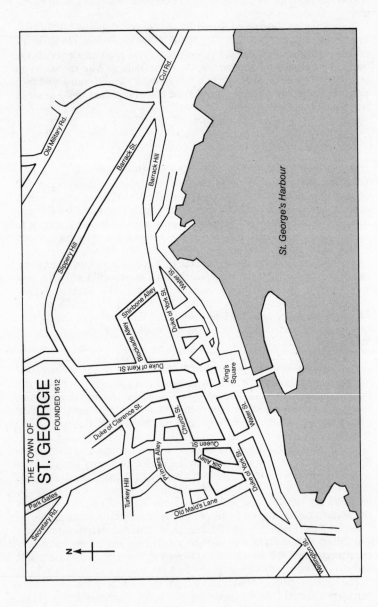

THE TOWN OF
ST. GEORGE
FOUNDED 1612

St. George's Harbour

King's Square

Old Military Rd.
Cut Rd.
Barrack St.
Barrack Hill
Slippery Hill
Shinbone Alley
Blockade Alley
Water St.
Duke of York St.
Duke of Kent St.
Duke of Clarence St.
Church St.
Queen St.
Silk Alley
Water St.
Duke of York St.
Printer's Alley
Turkey Hill
Old Maid's Lane
Park Gates
Secretary Rd.
Wellington St.

N

or spending the day in the stocks. Both, apparently, were accompanied by much jeering from the townfolk.

The beautifully restored Town Hall follows the lines of the original building that was erected in 1782 and is still in use as the administrative headquarters of the town. Inside, you'll admire the highly polished cedar furnishings, as well as a fascinating collection of old documents and letters. The top floor was once used for entertainment. Sign the guest registry and then pay a call at the Visitors' Service Bureau opposite. New and very instructive to the visitor is "The Bermuda Journey," a multi-media experience presented in the Town Hall, produced by the same team that created "The New York Experience." Bermuda's past and present are depicted with over 1,000 slides, accompanied by dynamic music and narration.

The *Deliverance,* a replica of one of the first ships built on the island in 1609, was commissioned by the Bermuda Junior Service League and launched as a visitor attraction in 1971. The original *Deliverance* was built on St. George's Island with native cedar and salvage from the wreck of the *Sea Venture,* while the smaller sister-ship *Patience* was built on Ordnance Island. These two vessels carried about 150 people from Bermuda to Jamestown in 1610. See also the bronze statue of Sir George Somers, unveiled by Princess Margaret on the 375th anniversary of his discovery of the islands.

Returning to King's Square, walk past the Town Hall and turn right to the old State House, the oldest building in Bermuda. It was commissioned by Governor Nathaniel Butler in 1620 soon after he convened the colony's first parliament in St. Peter's Church that same year. (Bermuda's parliament is the third oldest in the world, after Iceland's and England's.) The State House was the first building on the island constructed entirely of native limestone and was built in the Italianate style because Governor Butler believed Bermuda to be on the same latitude as Italy (it is not). The small windows and flat roof were able to withstand savage storms. Since 1815, when the capital moved to Hamilton, the State House has been in trust to the Masonic Lodge at an annual rent of one peppercorn, collected each year in a colorful ceremony in April. It is known as The Peppercorn Ceremony. This historic monument is now open to public viewing every Wednesday from 10 A.M. to 4 P.M. There is no admission charge.

Catty-corner from the State House is Bridge House, an 18th-century home that now belongs to the National Trust and houses an art gallery. (The owners of the gallery pride themselves on selling only art by Bermudians—enamel jewelry, hand-thrown pottery, prints by Alfred Birdsey, cards, and other work by local craftsmen.) The house is called Bridge House because there once was a small bridge in front of it, to allow safe crossing of a murky creek that has long since been filled in. According to legend, Bridge House was the home of two governors of the colony and was also a haven for an American violinist during the Revolution. Walking through Reeve Court and Pound Alley (famous for a murder and hanging 153 years ago), we come to Duke of York Street and the entrance to Somers Gardens, a former swampland.

To the left as you enter, a large tablet erected in 1876 commemorates Sir George Somers and his death in Bermuda in 1610. When Sir George and his party reached Jamestown in the *Deliverance,* they found the settlers starving so they immediately set sail for these newly discovered islands of Bermuda to gather more provisions. But the journey was too much for Sir George and he died soon after his second arrival in St. George. So, his nephew and companion, Matthew Somers, buried his heart in the vicinity of these gardens and took the body back to England. (No one knows for sure where the heart is actually buried, if it is, but here is the memorial and a lovely park named after the man who led the expedition responsible for the eventual settling of the Bermuda colony.)

A walk through the gardens and up the hill brings you to one of the most eloquent spots in town, the Unfinished Cathedral. This elegant Gothic stone structure was begun in 1874 as a replacement of St. Peter's Church, but work was abandoned after a few years because of a schism within the church and Bermuda's only cathedral was eventually built in Hamilton. Although abandoned, this unfinished structure has a majestic feeling and the cacti and palm trees that grow where the nave was intended add a certain poetry to the place.

Down the Duke of Kent Street is the Historical Society. Formerly a home built in 1725, this museum contains antiques that show how Bermudians lived over two centuries ago, as well as an old printing shop. In front of this building in 1801, a Methodist missionary named John Stephenson preached to blacks. Since this was against the law, he was promptly fined 50 English pounds and imprisoned for six months. Undaunted, he continued to preach from his cell window, which can be seen in the basement of the present Post Office on the corner of Water and Queen streets. Turning right on Featherbed Alley (so named because the inebriates used to "sleep it off" here), you'll pass the Print Shop, which houses a working model of a 17th-century press.

From Church Street, you can enter the churchyard of St. Peter's, the site of the oldest Anglican church in the Western Hemisphere. The yard itself is full of history and to wander among the tombstones is to replay the events of this small town. One of the most often-mentioned graves in this yard is that of Richard Sutherland Dale, an American seaman who was the last victim of the War of 1812. His parents erected the monument and inscribed it with their gratitude for the kind treatment Dale received from the citizenry of St. George, after he was wounded and taken from his warship to a local hotel.

Other tombs worth mentioning include that of U.S. Consul John W. Howden who was buried in 1852, a victim of a yellow fever epidemic. His gravestone reads, "We Shall Meet Again." In another part of the yard is more modern history. Buried here at the wish of their widows are the late governor, Sir Richard Sharples, and his aide, Captain Hugh Sayers, who were assassinated on the grounds of Government House in 1973. The assassin was hanged in the winter of 1977, a deed that led to brief unrest around the island and some destruction of property by a group in the black community.

The pride of St. George is St. Peter's Church, the oldest continually used Protestant church in the Western Hemisphere. The original wooden structure on this site was erected in 1617 and the present building dates from 1713. The handsome cedar altar was built in 1624 and the three-tiered pulpit is considered to be quite rare. The English-ironstone font is believed to be 15th century. King William III presented the silver communion service. The walls of the church are full of memorials to the town's historic figures, including Joseph Stockdale, the island's first printer, who died in

1803, and a much-admired governor, Alured Popple, who died in 1744 of the "fever."

Returning to Church Street and up Broad Alley (it was the widest in town), you can visit the Old Rectory on Tuesdays and Saturdays. A property of the National Trust, the rectory is a charming old Bermuda cottage built about 1705 by a reformed pirate. Its name reflects the fact that the Reverend Alexander Richardson, known as the "little bishop," lived here in the late 18th century.

Straight on is Printer's Alley named in honor of Joseph Stockdale, who came to Bermuda in 1783 with his printing press and published the *Bermuda Gazette* for 20 years. After his death, his three daughters continued the newspaper. The house in which Stockdale lived is now occupied by an editor of the *Royal Gazette,* the island's only daily newspaper. Nearby is Hillcrest, a large guest house with wide verandas and a moon gate on its spacious lawns. Among its famous guests was the Irish poet Tom Moore, who stayed here for four months in 1804 and wrote romantic verse to Hester (Nea) Tucker, who lived next door. Later, the Tuckers moved up to Rose Hill where the old St. George Hotel used to stand, a prominent reminder of glorious days and the once flourishing steamboat trade.

Two interesting lanes take you down to Duke of York Street. One, Silk Alley, also called Petticoat Lane, got its name in 1834 when two just-emancipated slave girls walked down here with their newly acquired rustling silk petticoats. The other is called Old Maid's Lane, because some old maids lived along here a century ago.

Coming around to Water Street, you are in front of the town's most historic old home, the President Henry Tucker House, which is also owned by the National Trust. At the time it was built in 1752, the house was not hanging over the street but faced a broad expanse of lawn that went down to the harbor. The house was acquired in 1775 by Henry Tucker, eldest son of Colonel Henry Tucker of the Grove, Southampton, and the husband of the governor's daughter. During the American revolutionary years, he was president of the town council and always in a rather precarious position regarding his family's loyalties in the war between the American colonies and the Mother Country. The Tucker family was bitterly divided over this war because two of the Tucker children were living in America, one in Williamsburg, Virginia, and the other in Charleston, South Carolina. Colonel Tucker tried to remain neutral but could not and finally became the central figure in a secret campaign to help the American colonists.

By the mid-18th century, Bermuda was dependent upon the American colonies for food and faced starvation if their ships were cut off because of the Revolution. Although most Bermudians were loyal to the Mother Country and had no desire to sever ties, they did not wish to go hungry. So Colonel Henry Tucker led a delegation to the Continental Congress in Philadelphia to beg that the supply of provisions to the island be continued without interruption. However, the Congress was not particularly responsive, since the Bermudians could only offer salt in return for food and the Americans wanted gunpowder.

It so happened that there was a large store of gunpowder in St. George and one mid-August night in 1775, the gunpowder found itself on two American warships that were waiting off the island in Tobacco Bay. When the governor found out about the theft the following morning, he was furious. Suspecting the Tucker family, he refused to speak to any member except his son-in-law, Henry. However, the island continued to be supplied with food throughout the war, and so no questions were asked.

Portraits of Colonel Henry Tucker and his son St. George Tucker hang in the museum/house along with mementoes of the family, which reached from Bermuda to the U.S. and England. Much of the furniture in the house was presented by a Robert Tucker of Baltimore, who died at the age of 102 in 1950. During the American Civil War, the house belonged to Aubrey Harvey Tucker. He rented his kitchen to a black slave from South Carolina named Joseph Hayne Rainey, who set himself up as a barber. (A lane outside the kitchen door has been called Barber's Alley ever since.) Rainey returned to his home state after the war and was the first black man elected to Congress.

Across the street is the Carriage Museum, where you can spend a delightful hour admiring the custom-built vehicles that traveled along the island's roads before the automobile arrived in 1946. The collection, begun by Mrs. Bernard Wilkinson in the late 1940s, includes everything from small children's runabouts to the most elegant and dignified carriage made. Many, such as the Brougham, Semi-Formal Phaeton, Vis-a-Vis Victoria, Barouche, and Opera Bus, are the type you've read about in historical novels.

The Carriage Museum is part of the multimillion-dollar restoration project that has been taking place along St. George's waterfront. Derelict warehouses, masterpieces of solid brick architecture, have been turned into a fine new eating place (The Carriage House Restaurant) and shops that are local branches of downtown Hamilton stores (The Irish Linen Shop, Trimingham's). It's a nice blending of the old with the new, and well worth a visit. Keep going. Another interesting block of shops and the Fisherman's Wharf restaurant can be found at the opposite end.

Back along Water Street again is the Post Office facing onto King's Square. This is the former jail where, among other happenings, the Reverend John Stephenson was imprisoned and continued to preach to the blacks from his cell. The barred window in the basement is supposed to be the cell in which Stephenson spent six months. The pink structure on the corner of the block is the Confederate Museum and site of the old Globe Hotel. During the American Civil War (1861–5), this end of the island sided with the Southern Confederates, not for moral reasons but solely for business concerns. The town of St. George became the focus of gun-running between the South and Europe, trading much-needed ammunition for cotton that Europe sorely wanted but couldn't get because of the Northern blockade. Headquarters for these activities were on the top floor of this building (which had once been Government House when Governor Samuel Day lived here in 1700). During the Civil War, the town's warehouses were bulging with goods and people involved in the war efforts became the "New Rich." However, this sudden wealth for St. George, depressed from the capital's move to Hamilton in 1815, did not last long and the town soon returned to its somnolent, debt-ridden state. The Confederate Museum, also the property of the National Trust, houses an interesting collection of exhibits about this period. A large wall map shows the major events of the American Civil War, as well as the blockade-running routes from Bermuda and Nassau. Also in the small museum is a replica of the Great Seal of the Confederacy and an antique press used to make reproductions, two rooms full of Victorian furniture, and descriptions of several incidents of the time—definitely worth a quick visit.

Before collecting your motorbikes for the ride to Gates Fort and Fort St. Catherine, stop for a minute at the White Horse Tavern, where customers throw bread crumbs to the carp who expect their three meals a day. This tavern was the former home of a man named John Davenport, who became very rich in the mid 1800s but had no bank in which to deposit his money and kept it in kegs in his basement. Upon his death, it took his sons several days to unload the cellar and count the silver and gold packed in each keg. It eventually amounted to over 75,000 English pounds, an enormous sum at that time.

Taking Water Street out of King's Square (past the old State House), you branch into Cut Road to Gates Fort, one of the oldest fortifications on the island, built between 1612 and 1615 under the direction of the colony's first governor, Richard Moore. Moore was insistent upon building forts because he feared attack by the Spaniards at any time. The fort is named after Sir Thomas Gates, who was on the shipwrecked *Sea Venture* and later became governor of Jamestown. Like most of the early forts, this one was originally built of wood but was later rebuilt with stone. The small fort still flies the Stuart flag, a relic of the period of English history when James VI of Scotland became James I of England. Around the bend are the ruins of Fort Alexandra overlooking Building's Bay, where crew members of the *Sea Venture* built the original *Deliverance* to take them to Jamestown. Ride along Barry Road by the sea to St. Catherine's Point, off which the *Sea Venture* was wrecked on the reefs, and Fort St. Catherine.

This fort on the northeastern tip of Bermuda guards the principal channel and all large ships, including luxury cruise vessels, must pass under the nose of these guns. This fort was also one of Governor Moore's projects and has been rebuilt many times, right up to this century. It is one of the island's major tourist attractions. The beaches on either side are considered close to heavenly. Not a shot was ever fired from this fort—perhaps the imposing sight of its fortifications was enough to scare away intruders. The fort is now fully restored and the underground galleries and magazines tell us what life was like in days gone by. A group of dioramas depicting scenes from the colony's history can be viewed in one darkened gallery. Upstairs, there are some replicas of the British Crown Jewels.

The long awaited 18-hole facility in St. George's is now available as a public course, operated by the Bermuda government. The course is open to all island visitors. It was designed by Robert Trent Jones, and has lovely views from all the greens.

Leaving the island of St. George's, one skirts over Severn Bridge and past the U.S. Naval Air Station to St. David's Head and Lighthouse Hill. This area originally comprised three separate islands, Longbird, St. David's, and Cooper's, but they were joined through landfill in 1941 when the U.S. government was given a 99-year lease to construct a naval base. The base played a prominent role in World War II. Needless to say, most Bermudians did not like the fact that almost two square miles of their precious land was being pushed about and turned over to a military facility. But time has healed some of the wounds and the story of Bermuda's role during the war is a fascinating tale.

St. David's folk are, by tradition, more individual and hardy than the other islanders because they live at the most eastern and isolated point of Bermuda. Also by tradition, they have been sailors and fishermen and even the local seafood in the unpretentious restaurants out here seem to taste better than in other places on the island. Shark is a specialty. If you wish to try it, stop in at the Black Horse Tavern or Dennis's Hideaway for shark hash. The turtle steaks and the fish chowder can't be beat, either.

St. David's Lighthouse has been seen from an 18-mile radius since its light first shone in 1879. Made of Bermuda limestone, the structure is only 55 feet high, half as high as Gibbs Hill Lighthouse, and some 280 feet above sea level. It offers visitors a panoramic view of the eastern end of Bermuda, including the three-island area that is now one (Longbird, St. David's, and Cooper's islands), the dramatic open sea, and the five-mile-square Castle Harbour, with its fascinating chain of islands across the entrance. These strangely shaped islands almost link Cooper's to the tip of Tucker's Town, which is also part of St. George's Parish. It is also possible to see Annie's Bay, Ruth's Bay, and Dolly's Bay. Smaller, but also in view, is Emily's Bay. Those must have been some women.

Leaving the rugged beauty of St. David's Island and environs, one again passes the U.S. Naval Air Station and Carter House, skirts around Bermuda's airport and goes over the causeway into Hamilton Parish.

If it's Wednesday or Saturday (10 A.M. to 2 P.M.), stop at the gate and ask the sentry for directions to Carter House, the oldest abode on the island. It is a delightful and unpretentious specimen of life over 300 years ago. Christopher Carter was one of the three men who can be truly called 'the first settlers,' for this tiny group remained behind while the *Sea Venture* sailed for Jamestown. (Washington Irving wrote *The Three Kings of Bermuda* about these men.) Carter was eventually rewarded with 510 acres of St. David's Island and his descendants built Carter House, where it stands today. The stone and cedar cottage was passed through the generations. The line eventually died, although Martha Carter Hayward lived to be 114. Later owners of the property raised Easter Lilies here. One resident left behind a famous ghost story. The U.S. military now preserves this charming monument.

Follow the Harrington Sound Road into Tucker's Town, which is also part of St. George's Parish. It was founded in 1616 by Governor Daniel Tucker, who wished to abandon St. George and build a new town on the shore of Castle Harbour. Apparently some streets were laid out and a few cottages built, but the scheme was never a success and Tucker's Town became a small, rather unprosperous community that lived by farming, fishing, and whaling. (Whaling was one of the colony's most important industries in the late 18th century and was centered around this eastern end of the islands. Even today it is not unusual to see small cottages with whalebone decorations on front gates.)

For 300 years, Tucker's Town remained a quiet and undeveloped area and, to say the least, unfashionable. But all this changed in the 1920s when Furness-Withy & Co., which ran steamships full of wealthy passengers to and from Bermuda, bought a large piece of the area for a splendid golf course and club. The Tucker's Town boom began as members of the exclusive Mid-Ocean Club decided to build residences nearby. The golf course is considered one of the finest anywhere, with splendid views from every hole, and the club has played host to world statesmen for high-level conferences. No one can buy a house in the area who is not already a member of the Mid-Ocean Club, and private residences have been known to sell recently for over $2 million, plus a 10% government tax.

Below the club and the golf course on the south shore are the Natural Arches, probably Bermuda's most photographed natural beauty. They are also among the island's oldest attractions and were popular for picnics long before the surrounding area became elegant. These spectacular rock formations were formed by the surf pounding for centuries against caves along the shore. The area has other lovely spots along the south shore, as well as in Tucker's Town Bay and Castle Harbour. The Furness-Withy steamship people also built the fabulous Castle Harbour Hotel on the other side of Tucker's Town, just across the boundary into Hamilton Parish, now leased by Marriott.

Castle Island was once connected to Castle Point, the farthest part of Tucker's Town. Governor Moore built his best fort—made of stone—on this island in the year 1612 and onward. As mentioned before, the Governor was worried about invasions from the Spaniards and it was from this fort that the only Spanish attack was repulsed. In 1614 two Spanish ships were sighted just outside the channel into Castle Harbour. Two shots were fired from the fort; fortunately, this scared the intruders, who fled to the open sea. According to the history books, this fort had only one cannonball left, and the early settlers could only assume that someone above was watching over them. The fort on this island was fortuitously placed and was constantly improved over the centuries. It even saw active duty during World War II. Only the ruins remain now, but the old stones have many interesting tales to tell.

WHAT TO SEE AND DO

A Practical Guide to Enjoying Bermuda

It is not possible to be bored in Bermuda, for this lovely island in the Atlantic has an annual calendar of events designed to entice visitors to return again and again. There is a super-abundance of activities from which to choose—interesting sights to see, beautiful beaches to relax upon, active and spectator sports, annual festivals and tours, and colorful ceremonies that have been tradition for three centuries.

Bermuda Rendezvous Time. Visitors to Bermuda during the "winter season" (November 15 through March) will not only find the weather perfect for golf and tennis but also a weekly program of free events to entertain them. These include a local craft show, military ceremonies, and a personal welcome to the old town of St. George by its mayor. All events are compliments of the Bermuda government and chamber of commerce.

Monday: Crossroads of the Atlantic. At noon, kilted pipers and drummers perform the skirling ceremony at Fort Hamilton. Afterward, visitors are invited to a Tea and Fashion Show at 3 P.M.

Tuesday: Bermuda Crafts. At 10:30 A.M. guides take visitors through the *Botanical Gardens* in Paget, and into *Camden,* the official residence of the Premier of Bermuda. The Market Day exhibition takes place from 1:30 to 4:30 P.M. at the Harbour Room, with Bermudian artisans and plenty of local crafts. Materials featured are silver, cedar, rafia, cane, sea shells, and plastics. The "Pickled Onion" pub serves complimentary draught beer.

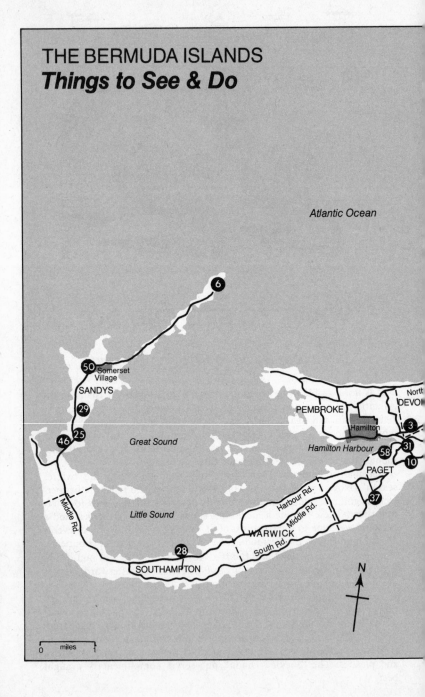

THE BERMUDA ISLANDS
Things to See & Do

Atlantic Ocean

Somerset
Village
SANDYS

PEMBROKE

North
DEVO

Hamilton

Great Sound

Hamilton Harbour

PAGET

Middle Rd.

Little Sound

Harbour Rd.

Middle Rd.

WARWICK

South Rd.

SOUTHAMPTON

N

miles
0   1

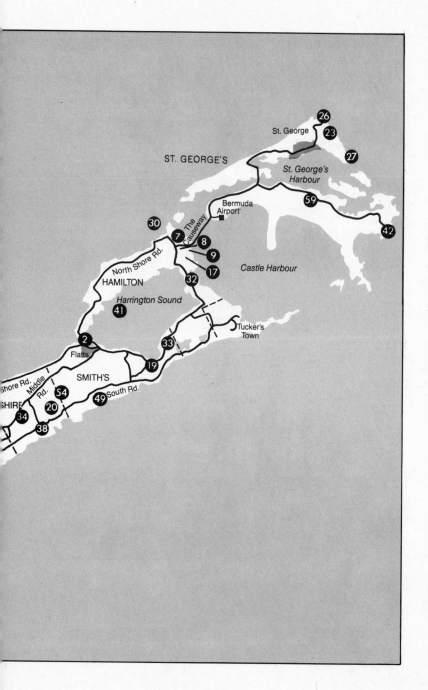

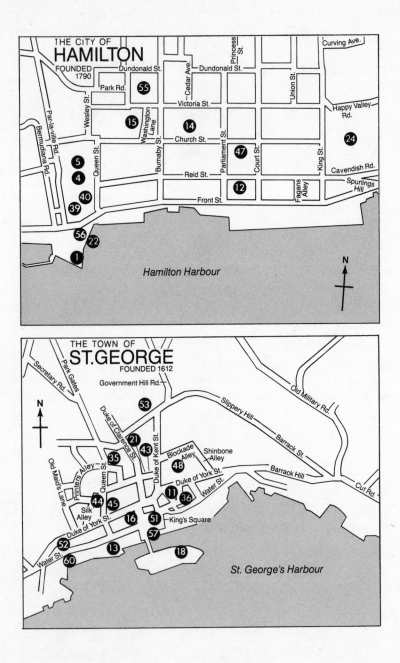

THINGS TO SEE AND DO

1) Albuoy's Point*
2) Aquarium, Museum, and Zoo
3) Arboretum
4) Bermuda Historical Society Museum*
5) Bermuda Library*
6) Bermuda Maritime Museum•
7) Bermuda Perfumery
8) Bermuda Pottery
9) Blue Grotto Dolphins
10) Botanical Gardens and Camden
11) Bridge House*•
12) Cabinet Building*
13) Carriage Museum*
14) Cathedral*
15) City Hall and Art Gallery*
16) Confederate Museum*•
17) Crystal Cave
18) Deliverance*
19) Devil's Hole
20) Edmund Gibbons Nature Reserve•
21) Featherbed Alley Printing Press*
22) Ferry Landing*
23) Fort Albert
24) Fort Hamilton*
25) Fort Scaur
26) Fort St. Catherine
27) Gates Fort
28) Gibbs Hill Lighthouse
29) Gladys Morrell Nature Preserve•
30) Grotto Bay Cave, Cathedral Cave
31) King Edward VII Hospital
32) Leamington Cave
33) North Nature Reserve•

34) Old Devonshire Church
35) Old Rectory*•
36) Old State House*
37) Paget Marsh•
38) Palm Grove Garden
39) Par-La-Ville Gardens*
40) Perot Post Office*
41) Rabbit Island•
42) St. David's Lighthouse
43) St. George Historical Society*
44) St. George Library*•
45) St. Peter's Church*
46) Scaur Lodge Property•
47) Sessions House
48) Somers Garden*
49) Spittal Pond and Spanish Rock•
50) Springfield Library•
51) Town Hall*
52) Tucker House*•
53) Unfinished Cathedral*
54) Verdmont•
55) Victoria Park*
56) Visitor's Service Bureau, Hamilton*
57) Visitor's Service Bureau, St. George
58) Waterville•
59) Carter House
60) Somers Wharf*

• Bermuda National Trust Properties
* Number refers to detail maps on overleaf

Wednesday: A Date with History. A day in the 17th-century town of St. George when the mayor personally greets visitors at 11 A.M. in King's Square, accompanied by the town crier. Members of the Bermuda National Trust take visitors on a walking tour of the old town, relating bits and pieces of history at 10:30 A.M. At noon, gunners from nearby St. Catherine fire the "Noonday Gun" and there is complimentary transportation to the fort.

Thursday: Treasure Island. This is the day to visit the rustic village of Somerset by motorbike, taxi, or ferryboat. Drop in at the exhibit of local arts and crafts at the Somerset Visitors Service Bureau, see the *Maritime Museum* in the Keepyard of the former Royal Naval Dockyard, stop on the way at *Gibbs Hill Lighthouse* in Southampton, see the beaches and the smallest drawbridge in the world. Complimentary tea is served from 2 to 4 P.M. in Somerset at the Visitor's Information Centre.

Friday: Sporting Bermuda. At *Port Royal,* Bermuda's government golf course, designed by Robert Trent Jones, join the weekly Rendezvous Golf Tournament. Camden, the official residence of the premier, is open again from noon to 2 P.M.

Saturday: Festival Day. Become an honorary citizen of St. George, with guided walking tours departing at 10:30 A.M. If it's your birthday or anniversary, enter your name on the scroll at the Featherbed Alley Printery in St. George. And get to bed early tonight; there is a run in the Botanical Gardens, Paget at 10 A.M. Sunday. Entry fee is 25¢.

Bermuda Festival '90. From early January to late February, Bermuda will hold her fifteenth annual *Festival for the Performing Arts.* Theater, dance, opera, classical and modern music are offered. Most performances are held in City Hall. Participating artists in past years have included the Vienna Boys Choir, soloists of the Royal Danish Ballet, the English Chamber Orchestra, pianist Emanuel Ax, the Lindsay String Quartet, and London's Philharmonic Orchestra. Last season, *The Fantastics,* the longest running musical in New York City, was the headliner. Seats to these performances range from $18 to $30.

Bermuda College Weeks. From March to mid-April, college students from all over will descend upon Bermuda for fun, frolic, and a host of government-sponsored activities. College Weeks began as Rugby Weeks about 50 years ago, when Ivy League rugby teams came to Bermuda to spend their spring holidays and compete against Bermudian and British teams. The girls soon found out where the boys were—and that was the end of serious rugby competition. College Weeks are an annual spring event and the Bermuda government organizes and pays for all of the coeducational activities. All a coed needs is an identification card from school, a return ticket, and written confirmation of accommodations. (This should include the name of hotel or cottage, meals included in the rate, number of beds per room, and name of travel agent for whom the group organizer worked.) Upon presentation of the school ID, each student receives a College Week Courtesy Card that entitles him or her to the daily free activities.

Each week begins on Sunday evening with a Get Acquainted dance at one of the major hotels (jacket and tie usually required for the gentlemen). On Monday from 10:30 A.M. (should anyone dare to rise so early), a big bash begins at Elbow Beach with lots of fun in the sun, a complimentary lunch, and entertainment by the Bermuda Strollers and other musical guests. Another beach party is held on Tuesday, with buffet luncheon, swimming, and the Bermuda Calypso and Limbo Festival. The College Week cruise aboard the *Canima* takes place on Wednesday at either 10:30 A.M. or 1:30 P.M. Complimentary lunch is served on board during the two-hour cruise through the islands of Hamilton Harbour and the Great Sound. Thursday is a free day (often another cruise to accommodate the overflow), and Friday features a steel band concert, complimentary lunch, and games on yet another beach.

Annual Championship Dog Shows. In March and November, the *Botanical Gardens* are host to every type of canine from Rhodesian Ridgeback to Dandie Dinmont Terrier. The dog shows are sponsored by the All Breed Club of Bermuda.

Art Exhibitions. The exhibition of works by local and foreign artists is sponsored each month at the *Hamilton City Hall Art Gallery* by the Bermuda Society of Arts. The gallery is open from 10:30 A.M. to 4:30 P.M., Monday through Saturday. The *Windjammer Gallery* and the *Bermuda Arts Centre* are two other good galleries.(See *Galleries and Artists* section. With a telephone appointment, almost all are happy to welcome visitors.)

Agricultural Exhibition. Every April, the *Botanical Gardens* take on the appearance of a state fair, with horse shows, culinary exhibits, displays of local crafts, flowers, fruits and vegetables, and livestock. The show attracts thousands of spectators each spring.

Houses and Gardens Tours. Bermudians open their homes and gardens to visitors during this annual tour sponsored by the *Garden Club of Bermuda.* For a donation of $7.50, visitors can see a different set of three homes each Wednesday between 2 P.M. and 5 P.M. (rain or shine) from mid-March to mid-May. This tour is a wonderful way to get some feeling of how Bermudians live in their own homes, with all the lovely cedar furniture and the famous "tray" ceilings. The tours include over 20 different homes. Chelston, the residence of the U.S. Consul General, is often included. Standing on more than 14 acres of well-groomed grounds, the main house sits atop a hill that is landscaped all the way down to the guest cottage and beach house. Tickets are on sale for each day's group at all houses and club volunteers act as hostesses, imparting charm and information. The tours raise money for the club's scholarship fund.

Peppercorn Ceremony. This colorful ceremony has been a tradition since 1816, when the State House (the seat of Bermuda government from 1620 to 1815, when the capital moved to Hamilton) was granted to the mayor, aldermen, and common council of St. George in trust for a Masonic Lodge for the annual rent of one peppercorn. The date for the annual payment of rent was originally December 27 (the Feast of St. John the Evangelist) but was changed to the most suitable day nearest April 23, St. George's Day, in honor of the patron saint from whom the ancient town derives its name.

On the day of the Peppercorn Ceremony, the regular meeting of Her Majesty's Executive Council in Bermuda (normally held in the Council Chambers in Hamilton) is held in the State House. The governor of Bermuda arrives in a horse-drawn carriage with much pomp and plumage, is welcomed by the mayor of St. George, and receives a key to the State House for the purpose of holding this meeting and upholding conditions of this lease. The key is turned over, the rent is delivered on a velvet pillow, and the members of the Executive Council proceed to the State House for their meeting. Members of the Bermuda Regiment carry the Colours (banners) of their Commander-in-Chief, H.R.H. The Princess Margaret.

their meeting. Members of the Bermuda Regiment carry the Colours (banners) of their Commander-in-Chief, H.R.H. The Princess Margaret.

Ceremony of Beating Retreat. This ceremony, which dates from 16th-century British military history, can be viewed on Front Street in Hamilton and King's Square in St. George's, and now there's a "sister" ceremony at the opposite end of Bermuda, at the Dockyard on Ireland Island. It is performed by the pipes and drums of the Bermuda Regiment and the Bermuda Cadet Pipe Band. Members of the band wear the Gordon Kilt. Some are as young as 13 years of age.

Bermuda Heritage Month. Begun only in 1979, the entire month of May is a series of cultural activities celebrating Bermuda's heritage. There are thanksgiving services in historic churches around the island, youth music performances, cultural evenings, and a heritage exhibition. The week of activity culminates with a festival parade from Hamilton City Hall on May 24, 1990, Bermuda Day.

Bermuda Day (Formerly *Commonwealth Day*). May 24, 1990 is a public holiday and the day Bermudians traditionally head for the beaches for their first swim of the year. It also marks the beginning of the fitted dinghy racing season in St. George's Harbour. And if this is not enough, there is a half-marathon (about 13 miles) race from the Somerset Cricket Club to the National Stadium in Devonshire.

Queen's Birthday Parade. A military parade takes place on Front Street in Hamilton each year to celebrate the Queen's birthday. The parade is scheduled for June 18, 1990, and places of business will be closed on that day.

Convening of Parliament. The governor drives up every year in November in the state landau, pulled by a pair of black beauties, to open Parliament. He is dressed for the occasion in full regalia, including a plumed hat, and joined by the Bermuda Regiment.

BERMUDA NATIONAL TRUST. This nonprofit organization, founded in 1970 to watch over the island's open spaces and historic buildings, sponsors an annual walk every Palm Sunday (April 8, 1990) to take visitors and residents through scenic parts of Bermuda not normally seen. The Trust is proprietor of 21 buildings and over 60 acres of open space, all open to the public. Note: Those who want to visit several properties can buy a $3 admission to a trio of Trust Properties: the Confederate Museum, Tucker House, and Verdmont Mansion.

North Nature Reserve (Mangrove Lake, Smith's Parish). Situated on the western end of the lake, just across the road from Pink Beach, is an area of living mangroves growing in a brackish (salty) pond. The pond itself is fascinating to students of water flora and fauna and attracts several species of birds.

Spittal Pond (South Road, Smith's Parish). This is the most spectacular of the Trust's open spaces and Bermuda's largest wildlife sanctuary. Approximately 25 different species of waterfowl come to visit here between November and May.

Edmund Gibbons Nature Reserve (South Shore Road, Devonshire Parish). Situated just west of the junction with Collector's Hill, this portion of marshland provides living space for a number of birds and rare species of Bermuda flora.

Paget Marsh (Middle Road, Paget). Special arrangements are necessary to visit these 18 acres of unspoiled wood and marsh land, which contain rare vegetation. Call Trust headquarters (292–6483) during the morning for permission to visit.

Scaur Lodge Property (Somerset Road, Somerset, Sandys Parish). This open area includes the site of Scaur Lodge, a Bermuda cottage severely damaged by a waterspout that came up on land, turned into a tornado, and drove across this neck of Somerset Island. The property is typical of Bermuda's steeply rising shoreline hillside.

Gladys Morrell Nature Reserve (East Shore Road, Sandys Parish near Cavello Bay). Two acres of open space donated by the Daughters of the Empire.

Springfield and Gilbert Nature Reserve (Somerset Road, Somerset, Sandys Parish). Springfield, an old plantation home, adjoins the Gilbert Nature Reserve, which was part of the land attached to the house. The building is fascinating from an architectural point of view and the nature reserve consists of five acres of unspoiled woodland, open space, and planting land. The finest rooms in the house are used by the Somerset branch of the Bermuda Library but are only open Mondays and Wednesdays from 10 A.M. to 6 P.M. (closed from 1 P.M. to 2 P.M.) and Saturdays from 10 A.M. to 5 P.M.

The prize of the historic homes and buildings owned by the Bermuda National Trust is **Verdmont** (Collector's Hill, Smith's Parish), a fine 17th-century Bermuda mansion containing antique furniture, china, and portraits. The cedar stair balustrade is considered to be the finest on the island. All of the 18th-century cedar furnishings are remarkable. Open Monday through Saturday from 10 A.M. to 5 P.M. (except lunch interval). Admission fee is $2.

Tucker House (Water Street, St. George) is the historic home of an early and distinguished member of the Tucker family of England, Bermuda, and Virginia. There is a fine collection of Bermuda furniture, silver, and portraits, as well as the Joseph Rainey Memorial Room, where the first black member of the U.S. House of Representatives practiced barbering as a refugee during the American Civil War. Open weekdays from 10 A.M. to 5 P.M. Admission fee is $2.

Confederate Museum (King's Square, St. George). The former Globe Hotel (1698) was the headquarters of the principal Southern agent in Bermuda, concerned with procurement and blockade running during the American Civil War. The museum houses an interesting collection of exhibits from this period. Open weekdays from 10 A.M. to 5 P.M. Admission fee is $1.50.

The Old Rectory (Broad Alley, St. George). This is a charming old Bermuda cottage built about 1705 by a reformed pirate. Open Tuesdays and Saturdays from 10 A.M. to 5 P.M. (except lunch interval). No admission fee.

Stuart Hall (Queen Street, St. George). Stuart Hall was built about 1706 and is now used as the St. George's branch of the Bermuda Public Library. Open Mondays and Wednesdays from 10 A.M. to 6 P.M. (closed from 1 P.M. to 2 P.M.); Saturdays from 10 A.M. to 5 P.M. No admission fee.

Bermuda Maritime Museum (Dockyard, Sandys). In the fortified Keepyard of the former Royal Navy Dockyard, this impressive museum provides an opportunity to follow Bermuda's seagoing heritage. The museum also includes a massive fortress designed to protect the British fleet in Bermuda waters. Open daily from 10 A.M. to 5 P.M. Admission is $4 adults; children under 12, 50¢. Refreshments available.

Crafts shops are being operated in an interesting Trust building. Mrs. Jill Raine operates the **Bridge House Art Gallery** (Bridge Street, just off the square in St. George), selling her own ceramic jewelry and the works of other Bermuda artists. **Tom Moore's Tavern** is another interesting Trust property and definitely worth a visit.

Any questions about the properties can be addressed to the Bermuda National Trust, **"Waterville,"** Paget (tel: 236–6483), where the director, William Zuill, sits in a cluttered office surrounded by a bevy of ducks and swans in the backyard. The whole scene is only fitting for an organization that cares so tenderly for Bermuda's historic property and open places.

SPECTATOR SPORTS. Bermudians are what one might call "sporting" and there are any number of sports events to keep visitors on the go throughout the year. For those who prefer to be spectators, there are soccer matches every weekend from September through May. Rugby and field hockey are regular fixtures on Thursdays, Saturdays, and Sundays from September through April. Cricket is the summer spectator sport, highlighted by the annual *Cup Match Cricket Festival* in early August. Watching the cricket competition between teams from the eastern and western ends of the island is only one reason Bermudians and visitors alike head for the Cup Match. It's also a time to show off new clothes and perhaps win a little money at the crown-and-anchor tables during the most colorful of Bermuda's sporting events.

Sailing: Races are held every Saturday from the end of January through the fall season by the *Royal Bermuda Yacht Club* in a variety of classes including Solings, International One-Designs, Luders-16s, 5–0–5s, Lasers, etc. The *Bermuda Offshore Cruising Association* holds races on the first Sunday of each month for oceangoing yachts. The beautiful Bermuda-fitted dinghies race approximately every other Sunday during the spring, summer, and fall, starting on Bermuda Day (May 24, 1990) in St. George and Hamilton harbors and in Mangrove Bay, Sandys. Visitors frequently compete in Sunfish races on Harrington Sound each Sunday.

The spectacular *Newport to Bermuda Ocean Yacht Race* is held in mid-June every even year, while the *Newport to Bermuda Multihull Race* is held on the odd year. The yacht race is the more glamorous and exciting and draws serious sailors and their elegant boats from all over the world. When the yachts reach Bermuda, there are plenty of parties to fete the victor and console the losers.

Also on odd years is a *Marion (Mass.)-to-Bermuda Yacht Race;* the traditional *Annapolis-to-Bermuda Race* is held on even years. Both draw racing heavies with super-serious racing by day and equally serious partying by night (which visitors have been known to crash!).

Powerboat races take place on Sundays from May through November at Ferry Reach, near the airport. Closed-circuit races alternate with offshore races. Marathons with top international drivers teaming up with local drivers are held periodically, and the *Around the Island Race* is usually held in August.

Game Fishing Tournament: The Bermuda Department of Tourism offers certificates and sterling silver pins for top catches of 26 varieties of game fish found in local waters. The tournament is open to visitors the year round. No license and no entry fee required.

In July, an invitational event draws teams from the U.S. and other countries for four days of competition against one another and a variety of tackle-busting fish.

Annual Goodwill Golf Tournament: This tournament in early December attracts some 100 American, Canadian, and British pro-amateur foursomes. During the winter season, there are many other golf tournaments sponsored by local clubs and resorts (see *Sports* section).

Bermuda Fifteenth Annual International Marathon: This 26-mile, 385-yard endurance race is scheduled for January 21, 1990. Sponsored by the Bermuda Department of Tourism, Eastern Airlines, and Adidas, the sports equipment people. This marathon is beginning to attract "name" runners, but everyone is invited to join. There is a 10-kilometer race the day before (January 20). Anyone wishing to enter the races may write to: President, Bermuda Track & Field Assoc., Box DV 397, Devonshire DV-BX, Bermuda. There are now race weekend packages available from Marathon Tours, Inc., 108 Main St., Charlestown District, Boston, Mass., 02129(617–242–7845).

BOTANICAL GARDENS. When hurricane Emily roared through Bermuda in September 1987, she took almost a third of the lovingly tended trees and shrubs with her. Nowhere is this still as dramatically apparent as at the once-majestic gardens. Landscape architects and volunteers are replanting, and the gardens will soon return to their former glory, with every plant indigenous to Bermuda on display, along with imported thousands. Stroll through the 36-acre landscape and have lunch or dinner at Tavern on the Green. Free tours are conducted from 10:30 A.M. to noon on Tuesdays, Wednesdays, and Fridays (except public holidays). The gardens are open daily from sunrise to sunset and the plant houses can be visited from 8 A.M. to 5 P.M. (except public holidays), Monday through Saturday. Admission is free.

FORTS. The first thing passengers aboard cruise vessels see as they enter the principal channel of the island is *Fort St. Catherine*. The stone fortification was built in the 19th century on the site of a wooden construction that dated from 1612. The first governor of Bermuda, Richard Moore, built nine forts at strategic places to prevent invasion from the free-roving Spaniards. Unfortunately, eight of them were wood and did not last, but the sites he chose were so strategic that stone fortifications were built upon them later.

Fort St. Catherine has been fully restored. Its underground galleries are used to highlight the island's early history, while a replica of the Crown Jewels can be viewed in one of the upper galleries. The fort is one of Bermuda's most popular tourist attractions. It is open from 10 A.M. to 4:30 P.M. and adult admission is $1, children under 12 admitted free.

The one stone fortification that Governor Moore built was *King's Fort* on Castle Island, to guard the entrance to Castle Harbour. Shots were fired from this fort at a Spanish warship in 1614 and she fled after two rounds—fortuitous, because Moore's men had only one shot left! The fort is now in ruins.

In 1834, the famous Duke of Wellington (who had defeated Napoleon at Waterloo) devised a scheme for the defense of this little island. It included the building of *Fort Scaur* in Somerset, *Fort Hamilton* overlooking the capital city, and the South Shore Road. Wellington's plan was to station troops all along this road to protect the South Shore, but there was never a need.

The restored *Fort Hamilton* offers a panoramic view of the city and harbor. Its old cannons still point threateningly out to sea and its musty labyrinth of galleries is open. One enters the fort from a wooden bridge that crosses the moat now filled with native flora. Walk around the moat and feel that you are in a jungle of exotic plants and birds. The fort is open from 9:30 A.M. to 5 P.M. Sunday through Friday (*closed Saturdays*) and approached via Victoria and King streets and Happy Valley Road. The less-energetic should taxi up and walk down.

Fort Scaur in Somerset has also been restored and offers a view of the Great Sound. Open from 9 A.M. to 5 P.M. daily, it is a good place to rest and picnic during a day's jaunt by motorbike to the westward end of the island. Sit on the grassy knoll and enjoy the sun. You will probably be asked to sign the guestbook.

Gates Fort, on the island of St. George's, was built between 1612 and 1615 under the direction of Governor Moore. It was named after Sir Thomas Gates, one of the prominent persons aboard the shipwrecked *Sea Venture,* who is said to have leapt ashore and shouted, "This is Gates, his Bay!" This smaller, restored fort is open from 9 A.M. to 5 P.M. daily.

CHURCHES. There are plenty of charming churches to visit throughout the islands. Their graveyards are a fascinating course in history. (Do not hesitate to stop and wander through each one.) *St. Peter's* (Duke of York Street, St. George) is the oldest church in Bermuda. Anglican churches have stood on this site longer than anywhere else in the Western Hemisphere. It is a simple, whitewashed building with highly polished cedar doors, floors, and pews. Its pulpit and altar date from the early 17th century and the font is believed to be 15th century. The communion service was presented by King William III and the walls are lined with memorial tablets to well-known Bermudians. The graveyard behind the building is also full of famous names, including U.S. Consul John W. Howden, who died of yellow fever in 1852 (his tombstone says, "We Shall Meet Again"), a young American seaman Richard Sutherland Dale who died in the last, and futile, battle of the War of 1812, and Sir Richard Sharples and his aide, Captain Hugh Sayers, who were assassinated on the grounds of Government House in 1973.

Not far from St. George is the stone ruin of a church that never quite made it. Known as the *Unfinished Cathedral,* it has its own majesty and history, even though it lies abandoned with only the palm trees for company.

Bermuda's Anglican Cathedral, on Church Street in Hamilton, was dedicated in 1894 but was built in early English style. It is a bright and cheerful church, with beautiful stained-glass windows that shine even on a dull day. One of them, the Angel Window on the east wall, was designed by a local artist, Vivienne Gilmore Gardener. A Warrior Chapel, dedicated in 1977, contains the flags of the armed forces connected with Bermuda and two throne chairs for use on royal occasions. The kneeling pads in the pews are all hand-embroidered.

LIGHTHOUSES. *Gibbs Hill Lighthouse* is one of the few lighthouses in the world made of cast iron. It was cast in England and brought to the island in pieces. On May 1, the lighthouse will celebrate its 143rd birthday. The light, which shines some 354 feet above sea level, can be seen by sailors as far away as 40 miles. The light is supplied by a 1,500-watt electric bulb (installed in 1952) and the perfectly polished brass mechanism that circulates the beam can be seen by climbing 185 steps. On a clear day, you can see forever, or almost. If it's windy, the timid should remain below because this lighthouse does have a reputation for swaying. Open 9 A.M. to 4:30 P.M. daily. Admission for adults and children over three years of age is 75¢.

St. David's Lighthouse celebrates its 111th anniversary this year. Located at St. David's Island in St. George's Parish, this stone structure is half the size of Gibbs Hill but equally important to ships entering the main channel. It's open to the public May 24–Labor Day.

CAVES. Four of Bermuda's fascinating caves, subterranean worlds full of stalagmites and stalactites and mirror lakes, are open to the public. Well worth the tour are *Crystal Cave* and *Leamington Cave* in Bailey's Bay, which attract thousands of visitors each year. The former was discovered by two young boys in 1907, a two-acre cavern with a tidal pool that is 200 feet long and as deep as 80 feet. A bridge was built in the cave in 1928. Visitors can walk along while colored lights dance against the ice formations. *Leamington Cave,* which was discovered in 1910 and opened to the public four years later, is not far away. Both cost $2.50 for adults; $1 for children. *Crystal Caves* is open from 9:30 A.M. to 4:30 P.M. daily. *Leamington Cave* is open from 9:30 A.M. to 4:30 P.M. but closed Sundays and mid-December to February.

The Grotto Bay Beach and Tennis Club has turned one of its caves into a romantic lounge featuring music of the 1930s to 1960s. It has cozy seating for 80 persons around an underground lake that is 25 feet deep in some places. Next to it is *Cathedral Cave.* The hotel offers tours, but be forewarned—you may have to crawl along. If you are an avid spelunker, you will revel in this sort of thing but wear old clothes and cover your knees.

HISTORIC SITES. A replica of the *Deliverance,* one of the two ships built by the castaways from the *Sea Venture* in 1609, can be visited daily on Ordnance Island, St. George's, from 10 A.M. to 5 P.M. The original *Deliverance* weighed 80 tons and was built from salvage from the wreck of the *Sea Venture* and cedar found on the island. It carried 130 people. This *Deliverance,* commissioned by the Bermuda Junior Service League, is open daily from 10 A.M. to 5 P.M. See also the new bronze statue of Sir George Somers, by local artist Desmond Fountain.

Carter House: One of Bermuda's oldest stone structures, has been restored and is open to the public (free) on Wednesdays and Saturdays from 10 A.M. to 2 P.M. The cottage, located in St. David's, was built around 1640 by Christopher Carter, one of the original crew of the *Sea Venture.* Passes to view this historical landmark must be obtained at the U.S. Naval Air Station (Gate 1) on St. David's Island.

Carriage Museum: The automobile only came to Bermuda in 1946 and when it did, the horse-drawn carriage became a thing of the past. Many of these fine, custom-built vehicles were saved and in 1960 put into a museum. In it are a surrey with fringe on top, a brougham, semi-formal phaeton, a hearse built in 1856 for St. George and used for over a century, a Victoria that came from the Metropolitan Opera House in Philadelphia but saw 30 years' active service in Bermuda, a buckboard, pony cart, dog cart, and more. The curator will let you climb into the carriages to dream of bygone days and will even insist upon taking your photo. Just focus your camera and let him push the button—it's fun to see when you get home. The *Carriage Museum* on Somers Wharf in St. George is open Monday through Saturday from 9 A.M. to 5 P.M. There is no admission charge, but donations are appreciated.

Perot Post Office, Bermuda Library, Par-La-Ville Gardens: Just a short skip from the ferry landing, around the policeman's "birdcage" and up Queen Street, is Hamilton's first post office, named after William Bennett Perot, the first postmaster. Next door to the post office was Perot's home, now the Bermuda Library, and the gardens that he nurtured are now a public park. A historical museum on the ground floor of this two-story building has exhibits of old cedar furniture, china, hog pennies (the original money of the island), as well as portraits of Sir George and Lady Somers, a copy of the 17th-century map made by Richard Norwood, who surveyed the islands and divided them into the tribes by which they are known today, and a copy of the letter George Washington wrote from Camp Cambridge on September 6, 1775 to beg the islanders for gunpowder to fight the British. *Perot Post Office* is open from 9 A.M. to 5 P.M. Monday through Friday and to 12 noon on Saturday (buy some colorful stamps), and the *Historical Society Museum* is open from 10 A.M. to 5 P.M. Monday through Saturday (except Thursday and lunch interval). Both are free for browsing and a bit of reliving history.

The Dockyard: Until the mid-1950s, this was a working dockyard of the British Royal Navy, which still keeps a presence here with representative troops housed at "HMS Malabar." A landlocked compound, it's still officially His Majesty's Ship! After Great Britain turned all navy facilities over to the Bermuda government, they began ongoing construction—scheduled for completion in 1992, to coincide with Columbus's discovery of the New World.

The *Maritime Museum* is the most spectacular of the restored buildings, housed in the base of the former *keepyard* (inner fortifications of the giant fortress), housing exhibits of Bermuda's seagoing history of over 300 years. A self-guided tour begins in the Queen's Exhibition Hall, originally built in 1850 to store gunpowder, and continues to the gun emplacements that surround the dockyard. An indoor-outdoor museum contains ship models, and the eastern building houses the Bermuda Fitted Dinghy exhibit, including the 17-foot *Spirit of Bermuda* built by two locals in 1935 to sail to New York. The Maritime Museum is open daily from 10 A.M. to 4:30 P.M. Cost: $5 adults; $1 children under 12.

Recently opened, the *Neptune Cinema in the Cooperage* is a two-minute stroll from the museum, and offers a first-rate multimedia show, "The Attack on Washington." The show takes the viewer back to 1812, when some 2,500 British troops sailed to Washington to tame the "arrogant Americans"—and they nearly did! The continuous show is on the half-hour, 10

A.M. to 4 P.M. Cost: $2.50 adults; $1.50 children. In the evening, the cinema shows first-run films from the U.S. and Europe.

There's also a *Craft Market* in the adjacent Bermuda Arts Centre that displays local crafts in informal stalls. Often, the artist who created the pottery, hand-dipped candles, gem tree of semiprecious stones, cedar rolling pin, hand-sewn quilt, or watercolor scenic is minding the store. It's an informal and entertaining way to meet Bermudians.

The newly opened *Marina Del Oestes* now welcomes private yachts, and the new clubhouse and restaurant is open to all visitors. While there may be one cruise ship in port, it will be only one, since a local (and very wise) law decrees that one is the limit.

Two nightclubs opened their doors here in the summer of '89, along with several restaurants. A cluster of boutiques of "known names" in Hamilton (Trimingham's, Smith's, etc.) have also opened branches, followed by nooks selling ice cream and pizza.

Our tip: After a full morning of discovery, buy the best fish sandwich in Bermuda at the *Freeport Gardens Restaurant,* a simple eatery at the gate to the Dockyard. Sample a "dark and stormy," the Bermudian black rum and ginger beer, then head to Black Bay Beach (off the main road). You'll know you've found the place by Turtle Rock, which juts out of the ocean and is shaped like a water-borne turtle. This is a perfect spot for private picnics.

OTHER ATTRACTIONS. The *Bermuda Aquarium, Museum and Children's Zoo* is located in Flatts Village, North Shore Road, Hamilton Parish. Here you can see all forms of the island's tropical marine life, natural history, and an amusing collection of parrots, flamingoes, and giant tortoises that come from the Galapagos Islands in the Pacific. A new exhibit depicts Bermuda's geological development in relation to the rest of the world. Open daily from 9 A.M. to 4:30 P.M. Admission is $3 for adults, 50¢ for children under 16.

Devil's Hole in Harrington Sound is a protected pool where you can fish but can't catch anything. It is billed as Bermuda's "first attraction" since the original owner, Mr. Trott, began charging visitors an admission fee in 1843. Open Monday through Saturday from 9 A.M. to 5 P.M. (Sundays and holidays from 10 A.M. to 5 P.M.), adult admission is $3, $1 for children.

Children and the young at heart will also enjoy the Blue Grotto Dolphins that perform five times daily in a beautiful setting on *Blue Hole Hill* in Hamilton Parish. Admission is $3.50 for adults, $1.50 for children 4 to 12 years.

SHOPPING. At home, shopping can be a bore, but on holiday in Bermuda shopping can be a delight—a thing to do when the mood or the weather moves you.

While Bermuda is not exactly a spot known for its shopping bargains, there are some very special buys to be made here if you know where to look and what to look for. It is possible here to spend as much or as little as you wish. For instance, a set of Outerbridge's Sherry Peppers (a popular Bermuda spice and a great gift) costs around $16, while a three-ply cashmere sweater made in Scotland will run about $300. Or for more "touristy" buys, T-shirts and "Bermuda" umbrellas will run from $10 to $25.

"Traditional" buys in Bermuda have become a little questionable, unless you've done some homework before your trip and know the price of your favorite perfume, china, or crystal pattern (when on sale). Many of the "40% Off" signs must be using the largest and most luxurious of U.S. department stores for price comparisons. The truth of it is that there is usually some saving (if only on the lack of sales tax). The decisive point is simply: are you crazy about it? (Beware: Bermuda Triangle T-shirts may wear thin in Boston or Miami!)

Hamilton

Bookstores are high on our list, since this is the place to find bits of Bermuda lore, treasure tales, cookbooks, guidebooks, even island romances that are not sold stateside. A new book, *Underwater Bermuda,* has sensational photographs and sells for around $35. Also look through the wide selection of cookbooks, complete with bits of local lore recipes for local foods.

The places to find these treasures in Hamilton are *The Book Mart* or *The Book Rack.* (Large hotel shops also have a few offerings.) Best purchased stateside is Neal Travis' *Island,* which is—or isn't—a historical fiction about Bermuda's beginnings that has everyone on the island guessing about who is or isn't among the "characters" described. It's best read while starting on your tan and on your pursuit of the "real" Bermuda.

Insider's tip: Prices are the same throughout Bermuda at parent stores in Hamilton and at stepchildren elsewhere.

For serious shopping, Front Street and the arcades off Reid Street in Hamilton have it all. In the spiffy *Emporium* arcade is *Portobello,* with European antique jewelry and collector's coins and stamps. *Esprit* is on the second level, featuring the usual sporty Esprit line.

Stefanel, at 12 Walker Arcade on Reid Street, is named for Carlo Stefanel, whose proud Italian family is putting his name on snazzy, upscale knits. Most are cotton, with a scattering of jersey knits, in sweaters, skirts, and leggings for women; cotton and linen suits for men, as well as cotton dress shirts and trendy sweaters; children's everything, from casual sweats to this season's pants, shirts, and sweaters, with the colors and crest of the Italian navy. Everything is from Italy in this upscale chain of franchises, with several hundred scattered throughout Europe and a few now opening in the United States. Particularly good are the patterned wool skirts (cut at the knee), with hand-knit contrasting sweaters—all in hot red, purple, beige, and brown. The designs feature unusual colors and patterns with international style. *Sisley,* also on Reid Street, is a sister shop to Benetton, featuring unisex designs with pizazz—and price.

Trimingham's on Front Street is a tradition that dates back to 1844, and this is where it pays to have done some at-home comparison pricing. In many of Bermuda's best stores (and Trimingham's is among them), you can buy an exquisite three-ply cashmere sweater from Scotland. There are some pleasant lambswool sweaters, and a few rather plain Shetlands.

Since we're definitely not opposed to spending money, we recommend Trimingham's for some smashing (very expensive) crocodile purses, Liberty of London scarves, and silk works of scarf art from Hermès and Carres. One favorite is an exact reproduction of a 1670 map done in a 27-inch silk scarf by Liberty of London. Great for you, and great as a gift. Also here are the interesting and unusual Outerbridge's Sherry Peppers to spice your soups, meats, or dash a dish not properly seasoned. Check out Trimingham's line of jewelry by their own designers, and also the "Railway Collection" of safari-type cottons in pastel colors.

Archie Brown & Son, also on Front Street, carries some of the higher-styled cashmere sweaters, bearing the "Barrie" and "Pringle of Scotland" labels. Look for their best-seller here—Barrie's coat sweater. They also carry the complete Jaeger sweater line.

The English Shop is also not to be passed over in the search for some of Great Britain's finest woolens, particularly in men's sport coats. *Smith's,* a rival in English goods, carries cotton knits by Murray Allan that are bright and light. At Smith's we caught an insider's tip on the care of cashmere (which needless to add, they carry): Hand-wash, with the tiniest bit of hair conditioner added to the rinse water for softness and sweet smell.

A few doors further along Front Street (#23–#24) is *Calypso,* started in 1949 by Polly Hornburg and husband John. Their theme is less conservative, more casual elegance, and it works. Polly creates many of her own fabrics and designs, which have impressed Saks Fifth Avenue into placing orders. Daughters Susannah and Lisa do much of the ready-made buying, and they have the largest swimsuit collection in Bermuda: Gottex; Solar of Germany; Jantzen; Yves Saint Laurent. They also have an exclusive arrangement with Louis Vuitton. Calypso has branches at both Princess hotels and at the Coral Beach Club.

The Irish Linen Shop in Hamilton is a pleasant corner of British reserve that shows Soueiado fabrics from France and hand-embroidered linen niceties. Everything is of the finest quality, delicate, and pleasant for kitchen, bedroom, or bath. But it's the original shop on Cambridge Road in Somerset, that's the true find. Here, ladies serve tea to patrons in a restored Bermuda home.

Upwardly mobile teenagers (with their parents' credit cards) go bananas for *Bananas,* on Front Street with branches at the Sonesta Beach Hotel and in St. George's. Sportswear is color coordinated in bright Caribbean colors, instead of the familiar Bermuda gentle pastels. And secure in the knowledge that every proper English person must have an umbrella (and it does rain in Bermuda, particularly in chilly winter months), the island has created the "Bermuda umbrella" in hot pink and kelly green, blue, or yellow. Best of all at Bananas, the prices are quite reasonable for these trendy tidbits.

Another haunt of the credit-card set is *Making Waves* on Front Street, with action sportswear (Yuarnet of France; Panama Jack shirts, skirts, and pants), and owner Doug Patterson's cotton "Bermuda baggies," attention-getting cotton shorts, exclusive to this shop. In case you forgot to pack yours, this is also the place to pick up a Boogie Board or Frisbee, or maybe a pair of "fish" flip-flops.

One of the nicest, most aromatic little somethings are the small bags of cedar shavings of the harder and-harder to find Bermuda cedar trees. Piled into pretty sachet bags these are great for closets, clothes, even sweater drawers. (Art stores, galleries, boutiques, and crafts markets all seem to sell them.)

Other tidbits with flair are found at *The Body Shop,* 22 Reid Street, in the Walkway Arcade. Owner Ellen Brown runs this franchise of the original English shop with her sisters. All three sisters are perpetually on the hunt for unusual items such as an herb "sleep pillow" with marjoram, thyme, and mint stuffing; wood perfume balls to place in closets or drawers; and soaps of jasmin, sandlewood, lemon, and rose petals. Ms. Brown is proud of the shop's selections, all of which are naturally based products.

T-shirt shops have sprouted since the cruise ships began making daily calls in Bermuda; some of the best styles are found at *Bee's Knees* on Front Street—ask owner William Frith about the ones made of English cotton with an "onions" design. Bee's Knees T-shirts are more costly than standard T-shirts but also more interesting and definately of better quality.

By consulting with a local fisherman, we were able to locate the famous Bermuda shark oil that can forecast the weather. The seaman suggested we try *Wadson's* (across from the ferry terminal) or the *Phoenix Pharmacy* on Queen and Reid streets for this $10 item. It is a time-honored Bermudian belief that maintains that the bottle is clear on a clear day, solid throughout on an overcast day, and milky on a rainy day. If you notice a swirl through the bottle, run for cover—that's a hurricane warning!

Quite a different aromatic matter is *Peniston-Brown Co.,* the perfume specialists on Front Street, Queen Street, and in St. George's. Besides a good price on your favorite French esprit of parfum or eau de toilette, there's a boxed "Perfumes of History's Most Famous Women," small vials which suggest the passions of Cleopatra, Mata Hari, Marie-Antoinette, and Catherine of Russia. Another boxed potpourri of mini bottles is called "Les Meilleurs Parfums de Paris." Included in the collection are "Ma Griffe"; "Cabochard"; "Turbulences"; "Cardin"; "Le Perfum de Paris"; "Monte Carlo." This shop carries *over 127* lines of French and Italian perfumes, none to be sneezed at! This perfume boutique also has shelves of gifts for under $10 and $20, that make great take-home gifts. Also, some lovely English soaps by "Chelsea" of London and Parisian Roger Gallet's sudsy French bubbles are available here.

Mexicale Rose on Chancery Lane, off of Front Street, is a closet full of finds from Mexico: handmade rugs, papier-mâché masks, mirrors, silver belt buckles and necklaces, clowns with smiles or frowns, suede jackets, purses, and belts.

The town has many jewelry stores, large and tempting, but smaller, more select *Solomon's Jewellers* at 17 Front Street, owned by Canadian Alan Porter, is the leader in fine pieces. Not only does Mr. Porter have many of their individual pieces designed in workshops known only by him, he also buys privately from Europe, and simply states, "We are the only jewelry store in Bermuda that won't carry anything that isn't real." And that includes a most unusual leopard pin of 18k "standard" yellow-gold and, surprising but true, "black gold"! The price? Expensive.

Not everything is precious metals and gems at *Lone Tree Jewels,* but almost everything is unusual. Owner Mary Walker scouts the world for finds such as her recent offering of treasures from Afghanistan—silver filagree and blue lapis chokers, bracelets, and pins. Above this shop (in the Walker Arcade on Reid Street) is a genuine find: *Walker Christopher Ltd.,* which was opened eight years ago by Kirk Marks. His years of European training as a goldsmith are put to work as he creates pieces that range from silver and gold dolphin bracelets to intricate necklaces and individual charms. He also has pieces created around certified finds of sunken treasures: a gold doubloon dated 1715 in an 18K frame; a gold ducate from the wreck of the *Akerendam,* which sank in 1725; and a pure gold lavaleer, dated 1400, with the portraits of Ferdinand and Isabella, in an 18K frame with 10-point diamonds.

While there are many stores offering English crystal and china, the leader seems to be *William Bluck & Co.,* on Front Street in Hamilton and in St. George's. Quality and courtesy run high, and sips of tea or coffee are offered to the prospective shopper out of the finest of imported china. Now if that's not incentive to buy, we surrender!

Worth the slight detour out of Hamilton proper is the *Thistle Gallery* on Park Road off Victoria Park in the outskirts of Hamilton. Owner Hugh Davidson is a Bermudian who tries hard to find the increasingly rare Bermudian antique "anything" that is for sale. He finds he must rely heavily on European and Oriental antiquities. Very special are the "Bermuda dinghie," cradles that can serve baby or a variety of decor ideas. True Bermuda cedar chests are rarely available and need an export license to be taken off the island. Several beautiful rosewood glove boxes inlaid with mother of pearl (c. 1870) from England, and an English checkers set for travel are also available. The present pride of the shop is a China Trade porcelain plate with the Romanoff crest made for Catherine the Great in 1780. If you happen to have any of the other pieces to the original set now scattered among collectors the world around, you can add this piece. Keep your eye on the daily "Royal Gazette" for auctions, the place to find the few remaining antiques and other treasures.

In London, it's called *Marks and Spencers;* in Hamilton, the official offshoot is named *St. Michael.* Nevertheless, almost everyone in Bermuda calls the place Marks and Sparks. Under any name, finds range from cotton jerseys and polo shirts to Scottish tartans sold the traditional way (by clan and by measured length). Knee socks, which are worn with kilts, are just a counter away. This is also the place to pick up last-minute gifts priced under $10, such as St. Michael's biscuit packs and assortments of mints, creams, and brandy snaps. High quality at a discount, from cashmere sweaters to woolens for men and women; what's "in" that week is what you find. Think shopping at *Filene's Basement* in Boston, or *Loehmann's* in New York.

St. George

In our opinion *Frangipani* is one of the best shops in St. George! First expect to encounter Nickolas, the store's life-size, cloth mascot, who's in his chair by the door, rain or shine, donning a smile and sunglasses. Then there are the clothes, many of them from Greece; intricate cutwork from Hawaii; cotton batik from Bali; and of course, here and there, a dash of Europe and Manhattan. But it's the cotton sweaters from Greece (over 100 designs in almost as many colors) that are right with anything. Pleasant sales help is an added plus.

The Cow Polly on Somers Wharf off Water Street is another delight. Here, there are some reasonable buys in cashmeres. There are also needlepoint original canvases, men's silk ties, and beautifully embroidered baby frocks.

Which Craft on Somers Wharf won our hearts with a wall devoted to gifts for left-handed people. Lefty scissors, rulers, soup ladles, can openers, spatulas, and boxer shorts(?). There is also a counter with "gifts for grannies," which include more top-quality English yarn than we thought existed and dolls labeled "Gombey" dolls, made by Marion McPherson. All the crafts sold in this shop are made in Bermuda.

Constables of Bermuda has Icelandic wools at their boutique on Somer's Wharf in St. George, and at their three other shops in Bermuda. This is the place to find heavy woolens in smokey colors. From skirts and sweaters to jackets and coats, these designs are made to last several lifetimes!

The St. George branch of the Hamilton-based *English Sports Shop* (also on Somer's Wharf) has sweaters and more sweaters. This season's finds are the Sherlock Holmes detective caps, made of sturdy English wool with either the crest of England or Bermuda on the peak, and tweed workman's caps from Ireland.

Unless you've visited Bermuda in winter months, January through March, you won't understand at first the small profusion of sweaters, scarves, hats, and mitts—all made in Iceland. The offerings at the *Chameleon Sweater Shops'* four outlets (South Shore Road in Paget; the Hamilton Princess; Sonesta Beach Hotel in Southampton; and the Bermudiana Hotel in Hamilton) sell the brighter colors of Alafoss of Iceland. They even sell the treasured yarn by the skein, with free patterns for the brave.

Liquor. We find that all over Bermuda, the law requires that liquor purchases be made in minimums of two or five bottles—when the U.S. law is one duty-free bottle per person—a bit reminiscent of the days of the 40 thieves. But, a law is a law, and on higher-priced liquors there is a savings although U.S. duty must be paid on all but one bottle per person. Liquor must be purchased at least 24 hours in advance of flight or cruise ship departure to qualify for the duty-free price.

Locally made Bermuda Gold Liqueur is an island favorite that should be tasted before purchase. Like many unusual new tastes, this may be an acquired one.

And should you think that, in Bermuda, all that glitters is gold, cashmere, china, and crystal, the big sellers—the really big sellers—are T-shirts and porcelain pieces that proclaim "Bermuda!" One unbelievable figure we heard for T-shirt sales was $25 million. True or false, the smaller-cost items certainly outsell the major big buys.

GALLERIES AND ARTISTS. In Bermuda the art lover is given the opportunity not only to view an artist's work in a gallery, but also, in many instances, in the artist's own studio. Here is a sampling of the different artists and galleries in Bermuda. When it is possible to visit an artist in his or her studio, please phone in advance, as sometimes the studio may be closed to visitors.

Galleries

The Art House. South Shore Rd., Paget (236–6746). 10 A.M. to 4 P.M., closed Sundays and during the months of January and February. This is a small gallery that's worth the visit.

Bridge House Gallery and Craft Shop. King Square, St. George (297–8211). This gallery carries a large selection of the works of some of

Bermuda's best artists. Here you can see the fascinating "watch montages" created by Joy Blackburne, watercolors by Joanne Birdsey Linberg (the talented daughter of premier artist Alfred Birdsey); moderately priced hand-crafted costume jewelry, and maps, charts, and designer cards.

Crisson & Hind. Front St., Hamilton (292–2561). Crisson, a Bermudian name, has combined forces with Hind, a transplanted Brit, to present unusual imports from the Far East and Africa.

Gayle Glass. 1 Tee St., off Middle Road in Devonshire Parish (236–4321). This glass-blowing studio was opened by the talented young Bermudian Gayle Sherwood Cooke, who studied and won awards in London. Her blown-glass creations are sold in several shops in Hamilton and St. George's, but the work goes on at this studio, a 15-minute drive from Hamilton. Major pieces (plates, which take the longest to create; glass sets, and vases) are expensive, but there are cheaper items, such as $10 swizzle sticks, Christmas ornaments, and true-to-life glass cats.

The Windjammer Gallery Ltd. 87 Reid St., Hamilton (292–7861). 10 A.M. to 5 P.M. This is perhaps the best place to start to get an idea of what the island has to offer artistically. Artists from landscape painter Diana Amos to sculptor Desmond Fountain show here. Also look for the work of other island notables such as Bruce Stuart, Sheilagh Head, and Graeme Outerbridge. The gallery's owner, Susan Curtis, is usually on hand to give her knowledgeable suggestions and to give you up-to-date information about Bermuda's fine artists.

Artists

While in Bermuda you can visit artists' studios to see works in progress and to purchase or commission one or two for yourself. This is a unique opportunity for a visitor to meet the artist who created a special find for an hour of interesting conversation. Be sure to telephone first.

Kathleen Kensley Bell. "Hungry Bay," Paget (236–3366). Although dolls are not usually thought of as "art," the Bermuda costume dolls handmade by Kathleen Kensley Bell are an exception. Each doll is handcrafted by framing heavy-gauge wire and adding papier-mâché, and after many weeks of sculpting, the doll is finally painted and costumed. Commissions are accepted; prices start at $150.

Alfred Birdsey Studio. "Stowe Hill," Paget (236–6658). Monday through Friday, 9 A.M. to 5 P.M. Seventy-seven years young, Alfred Birdsey is an island institution. He has paintings hanging not only on the walls of the Bank of Bermuda, but also at 2 Wall Street in New York City. Birdsey's watercolors portray Bermuda in its glories and subtleties on everything from prints to canvas. His daughters, Jo and Toni, also display here, but the national treasure is Birdsey Sr. Mr. Birdsey is a recipient of the Queen's Certificate of Honor and Medal, a recognition of "valuable services given to Her Majesty for more than 40 years as an artist of Bermuda."

Corncrake Studio, featuring work of Diana and Eric Amos. Ord Rd., Warwick (236–9056). Diana Amos concentrates on capturing Bermudian landscapes in watercolors and oils; husband Eric, using acrylics, is an interpreter of island birds at rest and on the wing. Phone in advance.

Desmond Fountain. Call for address and appointment (292–3955). Mr. Fountain is an award-winning sculptor who uses the ancient "lost wax" process to create his masterpieces. He makes fewer than 10 of each sculpture. A great variety of Fountain's life-size bronze sculptures is displayed throughout the island. Visitors are encouraged to drop by the studio (a converted church) by appointment only. (Be advised that the prices of Mr. Fountain's creations start at around $15,000.)

Carole Holding. 3 Featherbed Alley, St. George (297–1833 or 236–6002). Ms. Holding is known for her watercolors and views of Bermuda cottages and landscapes. When at her new studio in St. George's (former 18th-century slave quarters), she's often working on a small botanical watercolor; her large landscape watercolors are done on location. Shoppers will also find her botanical placemat sets at Trimingham's, Bluck's, or Cooper's, in Hamilton; her originals at the Windjammer Gallery and at the Craft Market at the Dockyard.

Graeme Outerbridge. "Sky-Light" Studio, Southampton (238–2411). This Bermuda-bred photographer captures Bermudian architecture and texture, from sand to steeple in original photographic prints, silk screens, and posters. Outerbridge has contributed to the *Day in the Life* series, a team effort by international photojournalists to picture one day in time in places including Japan, America, and the Soviet Union. A few copies are to be found in bookstores of his limited-edition book on Bermuda architecture and his new book of photographs of bridges around the world.

Mary Zuill. #10 Southlyn Lane (off South Shore Rd.), Paget (236–2439). Mary Zuill paints Bermuda flowers, cottages, and landscapes in her tiny studio attached to her home. She will accept commissions and design a painting that is "just right for a visitor's decor at home." Visitors are encouraged Tuesday through Friday. The studio is, however, closed December through March, during which time you can view Mary's work in the Emporium Arcade in Hamilton.

One last suggestion on where to view art in Bermuda: the daily exhibits at the Dockyard, in Sandys Parish, on the western tip of Bermuda. Here a Bermuda Arts Centre, started by a group of local artisans, presents stands of arts and crafts with many of the crafts people on hand to sell their paintings, wood sculptures, embroidered pillows, and hand-sewn quilts. Monday through Friday, 10 A.M.–5 P.M.; Saturday and Sunday, 1–5 P.M. Closed on Bermuda holidays.

SPORTS

Head for the Greens, Nets, and Shores

Bermudians love the outdoors and are enthusiastic sportsmen. They have built more golf courses per square acre than any other people in the world. They also love tennis, sailing, racing in power boats, fishing, swimming, snorkeling, scuba diving for treasures beneath the sea, riding and, of course, croquet and cricket. If you prefer to "spectate" rather than do it yourself, you will enjoy the annual *Cup Cricket* match in August between the island's two teams. You'll also find softball, soccer, lacrosse, power boat racing, and motorcycle scrambling in Bermuda.

Golf

Tennis and golf are year-round sports on the island and there are plenty of places to play both games. Of the eight golf courses spread around the island, two are nine-holers, including the par-three pitch-and-putt facility at *Horizons and Cottages* and the government-owned *Ocean View Golf Course* in Devonshire Parish. Each of the six 18-hole courses offers the player a challenge, with the *Mid-Ocean Club* and the adjacent *Marriott's Castle Harbour Golf Club* in Tucker's Town providing the toughest as well as the most scenic golf holes on the island. The *Port Royal Golf Course* in Southampton Parish is rated by the pros as the colony's second most challenging course. Port Royal was designed by the famous Robert Trent Jones and is owned and operated by the Bermuda government. There are approximately 13 tournaments "sanctioned" by the Bermuda Golf Associ-

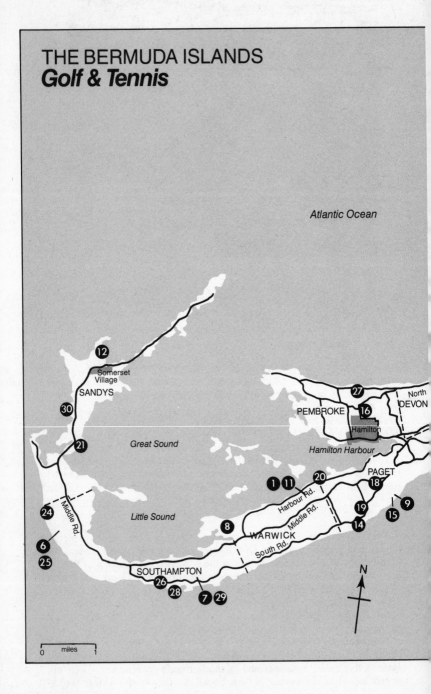

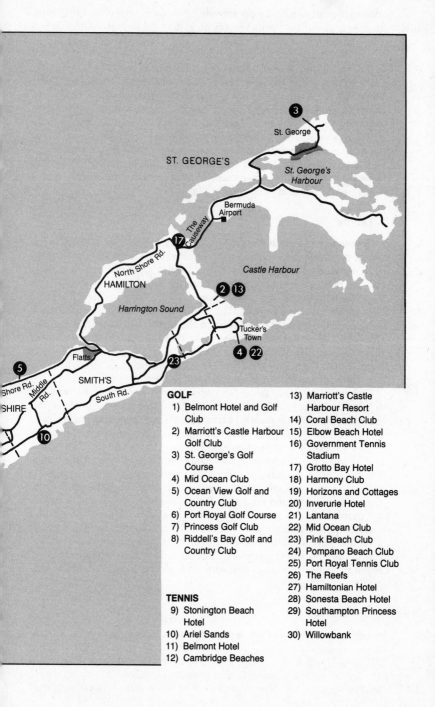

GOLF

1) Belmont Hotel and Golf Club
2) Marriott's Castle Harbour Golf Club
3) St. George's Golf Course
4) Mid Ocean Club
5) Ocean View Golf and Country Club
6) Port Royal Golf Course
7) Princess Golf Club
8) Riddell's Bay Golf and Country Club

TENNIS

9) Stonington Beach Hotel
10) Ariel Sands
11) Belmont Hotel
12) Cambridge Beaches
13) Marriott's Castle Harbour Resort
14) Coral Beach Club
15) Elbow Beach Hotel
16) Government Tennis Stadium
17) Grotto Bay Hotel
18) Harmony Club
19) Horizons and Cottages
20) Inverurie Hotel
21) Lantana
22) Mid Ocean Club
23) Pink Beach Club
24) Pompano Beach Club
25) Port Royal Tennis Club
26) The Reefs
27) Hamiltonian Hotel
28) Sonesta Beach Hotel
29) Southampton Princess Hotel
30) Willowbank

ation each year, of which eight are held between November and February, the official months for golf. Visitors on golfing holidays will find that the resort hotels hold weekly tournaments for their guests.

Introduction is required at both the *Mid-Ocean Club* and *Riddell's Bay Golf Club,* but not at *Ocean View* or *Port Royal.* The new *St. George's Golf Club* is operated by the government and was designed by Robert Trent Jones. All of the courses have well-supplied pro shops where equipment can be purchased, and golf clubs are for hire, although not usually in large quantities and not always in a full set. Golf balls can also be bought here as well as in the island's leading stores and cost between $12 and $20 per dozen. Between late September and early November, many courses reseed their greens, so it is advisable to check on conditions during this period. Some courses use temporary greens, while others keep the original greens in play while reseeding and resurfacing.

Tennis

Enthusiasm for tennis has grown as rapidly in Bermuda as it has in the rest of the world, and the number of courts here has more than doubled in recent years. Actually, tennis is an old and favored game in the colony, and has been a Bermuda tradition since the first lawn tennis court was built on the grounds of a private home in 1873. A year later, the game was introduced to the United States through Mary Outerbridge, who took some equipment and a set of rules to the Staten Island Cricket Club in New York. However, Bermudians boast that the first tennis tournament in the Western Hemisphere took place on their island in 1877. Tennis is a year-round sport here and there are many tournaments throughout the year for both top local and international players.

Currently, there are about 115 courts dotting the landscape, with approximately 85 accessible to visitors. The *Southampton Princess Hotel* provides the largest facility, with 11 courts, including seven that are available for night tennis. The *Government Tennis Stadium,* site of many matches played by ranking world tennis pros, has eight courts, and the *Coral Beach and Tennis Club* has seven. Both facilities are available for night tennis. The large hotels all have pro shops near their courts, where equipment and lessons are available, and racquets are for rent. The larger properties charge both guests and nonguests for the use of courts, while others do not charge their own guests (which is as it should be). During the summer season, the best time to play is in the early morning or evening hours. If a sudden rain squall comes, don't worry. Just sweep the water off the courts and they will dry quickly. One final note: Proper tennis clothes are required on all Bermuda courts, with white clothing and white shoes preferable.

Swimming

Bermuda has some of the most beautiful beaches in the world, with the cream of the crop located along the south shore from Southampton to Tucker's Town. Some are long sweeps of unbroken pink sand while others are divided by low coral cliffs into protected little coves. There are such interesting names as *Horseshoe Bay, Whalebone Bay, Elbow Beach, Job-*

son's Cove, and *West Whale Bay*. All of these beaches are easily accessible by bicycle, motorbike, or taxi. Changing facilities in beach clubs are open from mid-March through October. Swimming is enjoyable from about late April to mid-November, but the beach season does not officially open for most Bermudians until Bermuda Day (May 24, 1990), when local residents traditionally take to the shores.

However, swimming can also be a year-round sport here as there are a certain number of warm days during the winter months when the air temperature is in the 20s C. (70s F.). The sea temperature rarely drops below the low teens C. (60s F.). Many hotels and cottage colonies have heated pools, and the *Sonesta Beach* and *Southampton Princess* hotels have covered pools, which make swimming a year-round pleasure.

Scuba Diving and Snorkeling

Bermuda's clear waters are perfect for such sports as scuba diving, helmet diving, and snorkeling. Treasure diving has reached a fine art around the island. The hero is Teddy Tucker, who has brought up thousands of dollars of gold and riches from the deep. Tucker's greatest treasure is a gold and emerald cross that was recovered from the Spanish ship *San Pedro,* lost on the north reefs in the fall of 1594. Tucker and his partner, Bob Canton, have also recovered some interesting gold trinkets from the Spanish galleon *San Antonio,* wrecked on September 12, 1621, on the west reefs while en route from Havana to Cadiz. If you are staying at *Cambridge Beaches* in Sandys Parish (near Tucker's home), you will walk on millstones recovered from the English brig *Caesar,* wrecked west of Bermuda in 1818, brought up and laid on the terrace of the cottage colony by Tucker. If you're visiting the lighthouse on *Gibbs Hill,* you will find some old medicine vials from this same wreckage for sale at giveaway prices.

There are now several qualified, certified and government-licensed divers on Bermuda who also cater to the whims of tourists. *Skin Diving Adventures* are available daily from March to November. A favorite dive is over the wreckage of the *Constellation,* which plowed into one of the coral reefs to the northwest of the island in 1943. The ship was carrying a full cargo of cement, glassware, cosmetics, medical supplies, and yo-yos, much of which is still 25 feet down on the floor of the sea waiting to be collected by adventurous visitors. Contact: Robinson's Boat Marina, Somerset Bridge, Sandys (Phone: 234–1034).

There are also excellent aqua sports programs at *Southampton Princess, Sonesta Beach Hotel,* and *Grotto Bay Hotel.* Instructions in hotel pools, snorkeling, and one- or two-tank dives are available from mid-March to November (weather permitting). The underwater world here is fantastic, and should not be missed!

Water Skiing

Another popular sport around the island is water skiing, especially during the months from May to September. Water skiing is allowed in the protected waters of *Hamilton Harbour, The Great Sound, Castle Harbour, Mangrove Bay, Spanish Point, Ferry Reach, Ely's Harbour, Riddell's Bay,* and *Harrington Sound.* Bermuda law requires that water skiers be taken

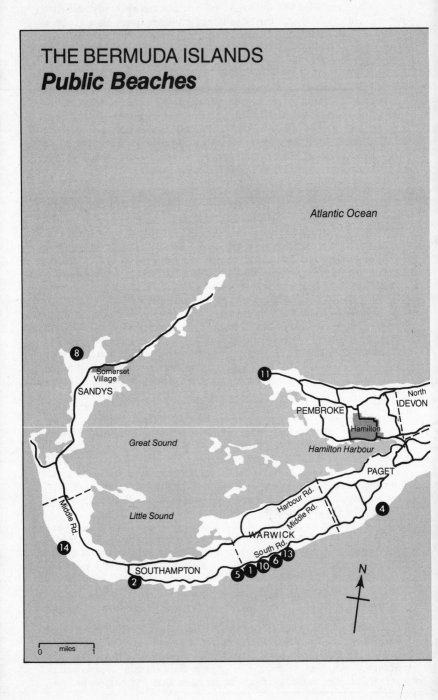

THE BERMUDA ISLANDS
Public Beaches

Atlantic Ocean

Somerset
Village
SANDYS

Great Sound

Little Sound

Middle Rd.

SOUTHAMPTON

PEMBROKE

Hamilton

North
DEVON

Hamilton Harbour

PAGET

Harbour Rd.

Middle Rd.

WARWICK

South Rd.

N

miles
0   1

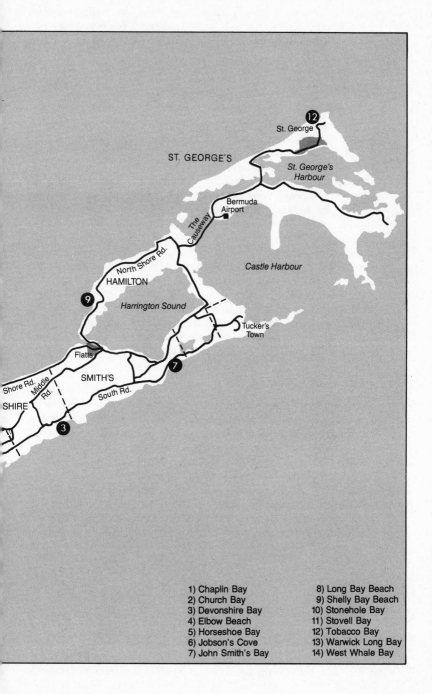

1) Chaplin Bay
2) Church Bay
3) Devonshire Bay
4) Elbow Beach
5) Horseshoe Bay
6) Jobson's Cove
7) John Smith's Bay

8) Long Bay Beach
9) Shelly Bay Beach
10) Stonehole Bay
11) Stovell Bay
12) Tobacco Bay
13) Warwick Long Bay
14) West Whale Bay

out only in licensed-skipper-operated boats, which are available at most hotel and cottage colony docks. Visitors who are not guests at these hotels may make arrangements with these or other licensed operators on the island.

Windsurfing

Bermuda's windsurfing champion, Hugh Watlington, operates the popular year-round *Windsurfing Bermuda* Glencoe, weather permitting. A 1½ hour lesson is approximately $35, board rental per hour is $15, and wet suits are available at $2 per hour. All arrangements can be made directly with Hugh Watlington. Phone: 236–6218

The *Shortz Windsurfer Sailing School* has two locations: one at the Palmetto Hotel in Smith's Parish (Phone: 293–2678 or 295–0339); and the other at the Sonesta Beach Hotel in Southampton Parish (Phone: 238–8122 or 295–0339). They are both open daily from 8:30 A.M. to 5 P.M. Instructors have certificates from the International Windsurfer Sailing Schools, with additional training in first aid and CPR. There are several lesson possibilities, the most popular being a two-day lesson plan of three hours each day at a package price of $90.

At present there's one other choice for windsurfing enthusiasts. That's the *Salt Kettle Boat Rentals Ltd.* at Salt Kettle in Paget Parish. They will rent boards at $15 an hour, with special day and week rates, or give a single lesson at $35 for an hour that includes simulator training and on-water instruction. Phone: 236–4863 or 236–3612.

Horseback Riding

Serious riders, or just early morning risers, find the Breakfast Rides at the *Spicelands Riding Centre* (in conjunction with the Warwick Riding School), on Middle Road in Warwick, an invigorating way to start a Bermuda day. Small groups meet at 6:45 A.M., for a gentle ride through nearby hills and along sand dunes behind beaches on the south shore, followed by a hearty Bermuda breakfast. Reservations are a must. Phone: 238–8212 and 238–8246. Riders should wear boots or sneakers, they will provide hard hats. The popular breakfast ride is $30; trail rides start from $15.

The lessons and supervised trail rides at the *Lee Bow Riding Stable* in Devonshire are for juniors only (up to 18 years of age). Adults are welcome on some of the stable's trail rides, $25 adults; $20 children. Phone: 292–4181.

Squash

Players will not be disappointed since there are four squash courts on the island, located on Middle Road in Devonshire. The courts are available to visitors from 10 A.M. to 4 P.M. by reservation only, made by contacting the manager of the *Bermuda Squash Racquets Association,* Percy Foggo, at 292–6881. Write to the association at Box HM 176, Hamilton HM-AX, Bermuda.

Jogging

This is a perfect sport for Bermuda. The tourism department publishes a comprehensive Runners' Map with five scenic routes. Try a "Run Through History" in St. George (2.9 miles) or "The Somerset Run" (12.4 miles). Races and mini-marathons are also scheduled throughout the year. One of the most popular events is the annual Palm Sunday walk, which takes participants through scenic, lesser-known parts of Bermuda at a brisk pace. Another is a Sunday morning or Tuesday evening "Jog for Fun" (the time varies), held by the Mid-Atlantic Athletic Club. Resident and visiting participants gather in front of Camden House on Berry Road in Paget. Check your hotel desk for details.

Serious runners should contact the *Bermuda Track & Field Association* at Box DV 397, Devonshire DV-BX, for details and entry forms for the annual January International Marathon & 10-K Race, and other special events that may develop.

Fishing

Fishermen with visions of barracuda, dolphin, wahoo, rainbow runners, almaco jack, and tuna will have some tall stories to tell about the great catch in the deep sea, off the reefs and shores of Bermuda. Fishing is a year-round sport in Bermuda but is best from May through November, according to the local residents. The *Game Fishing Tournament* goes all year, and visitors are encouraged to enter their biggest catches. The tournament, sponsored by the department of tourism, is for light or heavy tackle and 26 different species of game fish are eligible for awards when caught. Included among the most sought-after catches are Allison tuna, wahoo, great barracuda, and greater amberjack. Awards of sterling silver fish pins are made for catches that meet or exceed stated weights for various methods of angling, casting, and general fishing. To win the pin, you must fill out a special form supplied by the fishing bureau and have it properly notarized. It takes a bit of an effort, but it is well worth it, participants say.

Bermuda offers three types of fishing—shore, reef, or deep sea—all of which offer a variety of good catch. The most prized of all fish caught from the shore is the pugnacious bonefish. The best time to catch this fish is from early May to mid-July. Best locations for fishing are along *Whitney Bay* in Southampton, *Shelly Bay* in Hamilton Parish, the *Causeway* and *Castle Point* in St. George's. Other catch from the shore are likely to be: pompano, gray snapper, Jack, and great barracuda (during the summer).

As the island is surrounded by some 200 miles of reefs, reef fishing is a natural for those with some expertise who can look for yellowtail snapper, almaco jack, greater amberjack, gray snapper, porgy, redhind, little tunny (mackerel), and Bermuda chub.

Charter Boats

Skippered by experienced guides and accommodating from four to six persons, charter boats are available for deep-sea fishing with full day rates at $300 and half day rates at $175. Fishing parties are usually made up

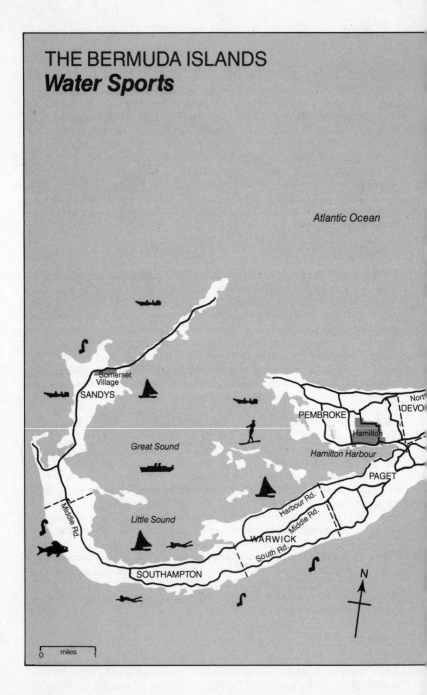

THE BERMUDA ISLANDS
Water Sports

Atlantic Ocean

Somerset
Village
SANDYS

PEMBROKE

North

DEVO

Hamilton

Great Sound

Hamilton Harbour

PAGET

Little Sound

Harbour Rd.

Middle Rd.

WARWICK

South Rd.

Middle Rd.

SOUTHAMPTON

N

0   miles   1

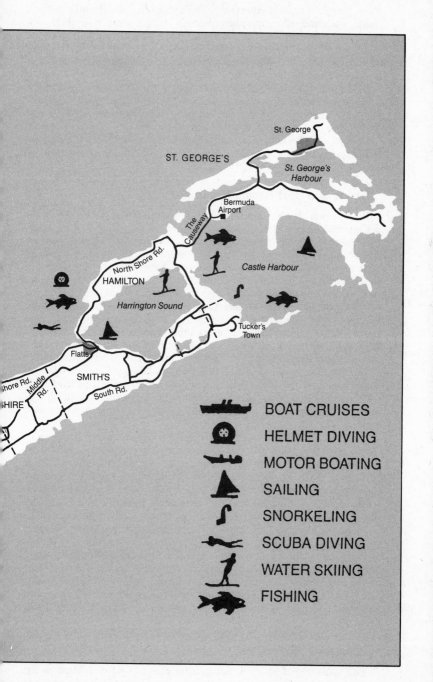

ST. GEORGE'S

St. George

St. George's Harbour

North Shore Rd.

Bermuda Airport

The Causeway

HAMILTON

Harrington Sound

Castle Harbour

Flatts

Tucker's Town

SMITH'S

shore Rd.

Middle Rd.

South Rd.

SHIRE

BOAT CRUISES

HELMET DIVING

MOTOR BOATING

SAILING

SNORKELING

SCUBA DIVING

WATER SKIING

FISHING

of six people. They are equipped with fighting chairs and outriggers, all tackle, bait, and other paraphernalia, but visitors must bring their own lunch and refreshments. (No fishing license is required.) Varieties of the larger gamefish in Bermuda's offshore waters are tuna, marlin, dolphin, wahoo, greater amberjack, great barracuda, almaco jack, rainbow runner, skipjack tuna, and little tunny.

If you plan to have a real fishing holiday around the island, you might want your travel agent to make all the arrangements in advance. But make your own payments in Bermuda, because windy weather may hold you up for a day or two (and you will not be charged).

Contact: *The Bermuda Charter Fishing Boat Assoc.* (292–6242); the *Bermuda Sport Fishing Assoc.* (295–2370 or 292–5535); the *St. George's Game Fishing & Cruising Assoc.* (297–1622).

Sailing and Boat Racing

Bermudians are also natural sailors, following in the wake of their ancestors, who earned their livelihood from the sea and built some fine boats from local cedar. Sailing and boat racing are probably the most popular sports on the island, and the turquoise sea is chock full of small and large craft throughout the year. From January to November, the *Royal Bermuda Yacht Club* holds races every Saturday in a variety of classes including Solings, International One-Designs, Luders-16s, 5–0–5s, and Lasers. In addition, the *Bermuda Offshore Cruising Association* holds races on the first Sunday of each month for oceangoing yachts. Smart, handmade, Bermuda-fitted dinghies race about every other Sunday from spring through fall (beginning the end of May) in *St. George Harbour, Hamilton Harbour,* and *Mangrove Bay* in Somerset. Visitors may also compete in sunfish races on *Harrington Sound* or in *Salt Kettle* in front of Reggie Cooper's *Glencoe.* Powerboat races are also plentiful and take place on Sundays from May to November at *Ferry Reach,* near the airport. There are both closed-circuit and offshore races. Occasionally top drivers team up with locals to race.

The real race is the almost 700-mile *Newport (Rhode Island) to Bermuda Yacht Race* that takes place in June on the even year (1990; 1992). This famous blue-water classic has as many as 180 elegant entries, considered to be among the world's finest sailing yachts, which sail from Newport on a Friday in mid-June and arrive in Bermuda within three or four days. This is a most prestigious event and "race week" in Bermuda is like Derby Week in London or Grand Prix week in Monte Carlo. There are other races on the alternate odd years, but none are so exciting as the Newport to Bermuda competition.

For visitors who want to enjoy the sea and the sun in a more leisurely way, there are several types of boats for rent by the hour or the day. Most of the large hotels have their own equipment for the use of their guests, and it is sometimes available to other visitors upon request. Sail along with the wind and the waves; it's all a part of the wonderful sporting life in Bermuda.

Submarine "Enterprise"

The submarine *Enterprise* was built in Europe and christened in the summer of 1988. Designer-owner-captain Beau Evans (of Looking Glass

Cruises) skippers passengers daily on submarine dives to the deep. Departing from St. George Town Square, the *Enterprise* operates hourly from noon, including night dives, to depths of 250 feet. Reservations are an absolute must (236–8000).

STAYING IN BERMUDA

From Hotels to Cottage Colonies

Whatever type of accommodations you choose in Bermuda, you will find it comfortable and pleasant and the service efficient. The island's guest properties are of high quality, whether casual and informal housekeeping cottages or the sophisticated and luxurious resort hotels that are practically self-contained villages. You can choose a place to stay from a list of over 100 properties, including the typically Bermudian cottage colonies and small guest houses that accommodate less than a dozen guests.

Cottage colonies are uniquely Bermudian—and are also the most up-scale accommodations on the island. They all feature a main clubhouse with dining room and bar. Private cottages are clustered throughout lush, green grounds, landscaped with both subtropical and tropical plants. The cottages provide guests with privacy while the clubhouse, pool, and tennis courts offer opportunities to mingle with other guests. Some of the cottages have kitchenettes where a maid fixes breakfast to be served on a private patio or terrace. There's a small refrigerator or bar set up for self-service. Guests' dining and nightlife revolves around the main clubhouse or poolside bar, as the colonies are quite secluded, and guests usually form a club-like atmosphere, under the tutelage of the owner-manager, an on-site Bermuda expert.

Large resort hotels have their own beaches or beach clubs, pools, tennis, and golf facilities. They also offer other resort amenities, such as night-clubs and entertainment, room service, social directors who plan activities, shopping arcades, beauty salons and saunas, cycle liveries, taxi stands, and a choice of bars and restaurants. In public rooms in the evening, gentlemen are expected to wear jacket and tie.

The smaller hotels offer much the same service, but with less activities and entertainment, and they usually have no shops or beauty salons.

There are housekeeping cottages and apartments throughout the island. The cottages and apartmentlike units all have cooking facilities. The owners will guide you to the local supermarket, which generally delivers, and will give you a bill for the groceries you buy at the end of your stay. Some of the cottages have their own terraces and pools and the larger properties are situated along beachfronts. These accommodations are excellent for families with small children. Babysitting can be easily arranged.

Most of the large guest houses are old Bermuda mansions that have been modernized to offer spacious bedrooms, dining rooms, and lounges. Some have added other units in garden settings. The smaller guest houses are generally private homes that can accommodate fewer than 12 guests. The only meal offered is usually breakfast, so you are free to try Bermuda's fine restaurants in the evening. Some of these guest houses are located on the water.

If you are planning to stay in Bermuda more than a month, it is possible to rent a private residence through a local real estate agent. Approximate prices range from $900 to $2,000 for a one-bedroom property; $1,500 to $3,000 for a two-bedroom home, and $2,500 to $4,000 for three bedrooms, per month. Maid service, food, and utilities are extra.

To receive a vacation kit or a free packet of information on staying in Bermuda write to the Bermuda Department of Tourism, 310 Madison Ave., New York, N.Y. 10017, or call 1–800–BERMUDA. For assistance in planning your trip call 800–223–6106 or 800–223–6107 (NY State only).

What Will It Cost? Bermuda has two seasons: A long summer, or "high season," that lasts from April 1 through November 15, and a winter, or "low season," that covers the months of December through March. Hotel rates differ greatly between these two seasons and you can find reductions of as much as 40 percent during the winter. There are, however, year-round packages at many of the island's properties that are excellent buys and bring your daily cost down considerably. There are golf specials as well as tennis, honeymoon, family, scuba diving, and other types of packages that feature accommodations plus two meals daily, sightseeing tours, transfers to and from the airport, complimentary tennis or golf, etc.

Prices quoted for Bermuda hotels and cottage colonies are MAP (Modified American Plan) and feature breakfast and dinner only. In some instances, exchange dining can be arranged between hotels with the same ownership and other properties may give their guests chits to dine outside, but you must pay transportation and the overage charges. Many properties in Bermuda are also offering BP (Bermuda Plan, with full breakfast only) or EP (European Plan—no meals) because rates are rising out of sight. Prices quoted in brochures do not include 6 percent Bermuda tax or service charges. The island-wide service charge is 10 percent per person, per day to the bill. *Many Bermuda Hotels now accept credit cards for payment.* If they do not, your bill must be paid in cash, traveler's checks, or by personal check (prearranged with the management).

Large Resort Hotels: Prices vary among them, but you can expect to pay from $99 to over $188 MAP per person (double occupancy) per day in high season. Low season 1989/90 rates from mid-November to April are about 20 percent less for MAP.

Small Resort Hotels: The 12 small hotels range in price from $60 (EP) to $138 (MAP) per person (double occupancy) per day in high season. Low season 1989/90 rates are somewhat less from December 1 to March. The plan is either EP or MAP.

Cottage Colonies: There are 8 cottage colonies, all with main clubhouse and cottages spread around lovely grounds. The rates range from $57 to $180 per person (double occupancy) per day in high season. The plan is generally MAP.

Clubs: There are 2 private clubs in the luxury category and require introduction by a member. They are the *Coral Beach and Tennis Club* and the *Mid-Ocean Club.* Prices on request.

Housekeeping Cottages and Apartments (large): These are efficiency units. The average rates range from $30 per day (no meals) to $84 per person (double occupancy). Low season rates are about 30 percent less.

Housekeeping Cottages and Apartments (small): The rates are from about $25 to $45 per person (double occupancy) with no meals, for apartments/cottages for four to six people. Most of these properties have a swimming pool or waterfront or are near a public beach. None has evening entertainment. Prices are less in winter, although many are closed.

Guest Houses: Prices and plans vary from EP (no meals) for about $30 per person per day; however, some places also offer plans that include breakfast. Prices are much lower in winter. As these places have no sports facilities, they will appeal to those who are not interested in the outdoor life Bermuda has to offer or those on a tight budget.

It is best to describe the many properties in Bermuda in the classifications the hotel association has given them, i.e., by type and size. All of the properties can be described as "top class," although some are more luxurious and more expensive than others. And readers must forgive the occasional oohs and aahs that appear in these descriptions, for although the food can occasionally disappoint, the settings of some of these places are unparalleled and the owners deserve several stars for the imaginative use of the landscape.

ACCOMMODATIONS

(Note: * denotes credit cards accepted.)

Large Resort Hotels

*Belmont Hotel & Golf Club, Box WK 251, Warwick WK-BX (800–223–5672). Situated atop 110 acres overlooking Hamilton Harbour and the Great Sound, this well-established resort hotel does not seem as though it accommodates more than 400 guests who can play golf out the side door, and tennis a few steps down from the terrace or swim in a vast, heated salt-water pool. Make the steep climb down to the ferry dock and you can catch the boat to Hamilton, a picturesque 15 minutes away ($1). A bevy of activities is arranged each week by the social hostess and there is entertainment nightly in the lounges. The 18-hole course is superb, the

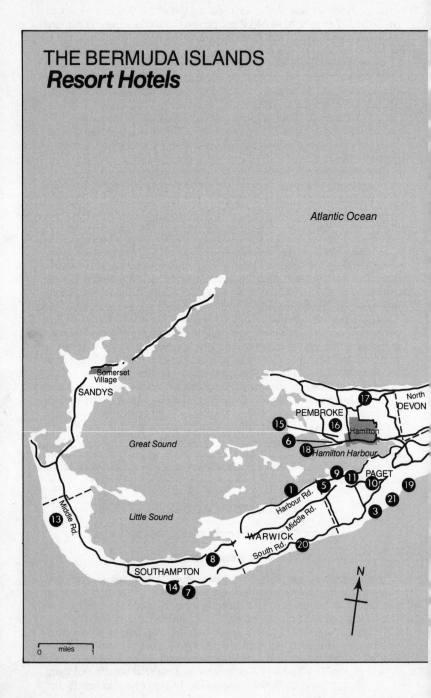

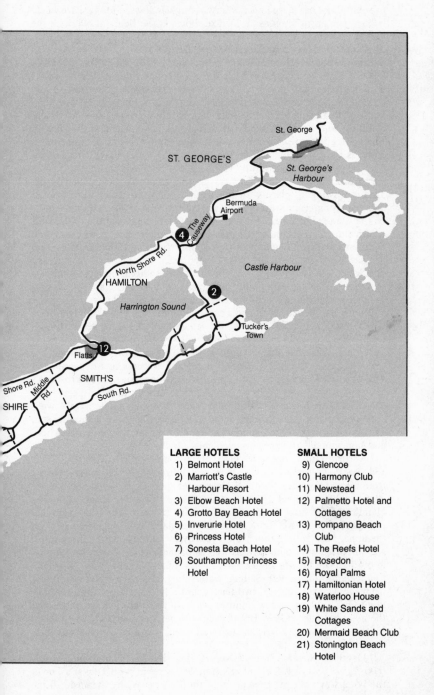

LARGE HOTELS
1) Belmont Hotel
2) Marriott's Castle Harbour Resort
3) Elbow Beach Hotel
4) Grotto Bay Beach Hotel
5) Inverurie Hotel
6) Princess Hotel
7) Sonesta Beach Hotel
8) Southampton Princess Hotel

SMALL HOTELS
9) Glencoe
10) Harmony Club
11) Newstead
12) Palmetto Hotel and Cottages
13) Pompano Beach Club
14) The Reefs Hotel
15) Rosedon
16) Royal Palms
17) Hamiltonian Hotel
18) Waterloo House
19) White Sands and Cottages
20) Mermaid Beach Club
21) Stonington Beach Hotel

Sapphire Pool has large underwater viewing windows, and there are weekly barbecue parties in season. Deluxe rooms at the Belmont overlook the harbor; moderate ones view the green hillside. This is a place for the cost-conscious, with good packages. (*MAP; BP; EP*)

Elbow Beach Hotel, Paget. Box HM 455, Hamilton HM-BX (800–223–7434). This hotel has come a long way since its beginnings as a small guest house in 1908. It's now a full-service hotel, the most solidly booked property on the island, even in the "off" winter season. The main house is situated on the crest of a hill that sweeps down to a glorious beach, complete with beach pavilion and deluxe surf-side lanais that overlook it. The 1,060 guests are accommodated in the main house as well as in private cottages and lanais that dot the 34-acre property, much like a cottage colony. The property is beautifully landscaped. If you don't want to walk up and down the hills, a mini-bus travels the service road to pick you up. This is a swinging place with five tennis courts, plenty of water sports, and nightly entertainment in the *Seahorse Pub,* one of the nicest "in" spots on the island. The resort is in a constant state of rejuvenation, with a new health club, dancing under the stars on the beach terrace, game room, and children's playground and pool. Two tennis courts and some gardens were just sacrificed for more cottages. Elbow Beach is a place where you can do a lot or a little, but whatever you do, it'll be in luxurious surroundings. Honeymoon, tennis, and family packages available. There are special programs for children during July and August. (*MAP; BP*)

Grotto Bay Beach Hotel and Tennis Club, 11 Blue Hole Hill, Hamilton CR-04 (800–221–1294). One of the smallest of the large resort hotels, Grotto Bay is a series of modern townhouse-type structures laid out along the ocean's edge. All nine "lodges" have private balconies overlooking the sea. The property encompasses 21 acres and features lots of tennis and water sports. There are two underground "grottos," one called Prospero's Cave, with 1930s to 1960s recordings. The other can be inspected (on bended knee) during the day. The main house is modern and well-appointed and a large swimming pool is just a hop from a small beach. This hotel is perfect for the honeymoon crowd. Tennis, family, vacation, and honeymoon packages are available. (*MAP; BP*)

Inverurie Hotel, Box HM 1189, Hamilton HM-EX (296–1000). This 134-room resort relies heavily on its social director to keep guests moving from bingo to movies, with full-scale water sports in between. On the understandably cramped grounds, it sits beside Darrell's Wharf, where the Hamilton ferry stops for the 10-minute ride to town. The club offers free transportation to two south shore beaches daily, a Roman bath pool on the upper level with harbor view, cycle livery and taxi stand on premises, and imported entertainment, as well as dancing in *Le Cabaret Nightclub* or outdoors on the *Marine Terrace.* Pleasant harbor views from *Salt Kettle Lounge* and *Marine Bar.* Sailing, waterskiing, and deep-water swimming from the Marine Terrace, two tennis courts free for guests, and the Belmont Golf Club just a few minutes' walk up the road. During off season, the hotel has offered "Fly Home Free" to guests staying at least 7 nights. Inverurie is a good hotel but definitely needs the announced renovation that they've said is coming soon. (*MAP*)

*Marriott's Castle Harbour Resort, Box HM 841, Hamilton HM-CX (800–228–9290). A world unto itself on 250 acres in posh Tucker's Town, the hotel was built for passengers of the Furness-Withy Steamship Line in the early 1930s. There is plenty of old-age splendor as you walk through the door. The property reopened recently following a $50-million renovation, which included a new 120-room terraced wing overlooking the waterfront. An elaborate landscaping scheme, refurbishing all existing guest rooms, restaurants and public rooms, a 700-seat ballroom, and a swimming pool were also added. In addition to 415 guest rooms and expanded convention facilities, the property boasts an excellent 18-hole golf course, private beaches, three swimming pools, six all-weather tennis courts, a yacht club and marina. A plus is the Japanese restaurant *Mikado,* with sushi and teriyaki prepared tableside. It all sounds wonderful and just what the grande dame of Bermuda resorts deserves! Good golf, tennis, and honeymoon packages available. (*MAP; BP; EP*)

   *The Princess Hotel, Box HM 837, Hamilton HM-CX (800–223–1818). Named after Princess Louise, the daughter of Queen Victoria, who came to the island for the winter of 1883, this was the colony's first and foremost hotel for many decades. The site has been considerably rebuilt since the 19th century and a $20-million refurbishing has just been completed to coincide with Southampton Princess's own renovation. The Princess is in the pink and offers convenience to town (five-minute walk), lovely views of the harbor, and all the sports privileges of the Southampton Princess. Complimentary ferry service between the two hotels carries guests for golf, swimming, tennis, and exchange dining. The Princess has all the amenities of a large hotel (shopping arcade, beauty shops, etc.) and two swimming pools on the water's edge. Fishing, sailing, and water sports can be arranged from the Princess's private dock. Guests may dine in the *Three Crowns* or *Tiara Room* restaurants or enjoy informal buffet lunches and dinners daily in *The Colony Pub.* There is a Mediterranean atmosphere in *Harley's,* and dancing in the *Gazebo Lounge.* This is a large hotel (1,000 guests) that feels large. It's good for groups and individual guests, with many package possibilities. (*EP*)

   *Sonesta Beach Hotel, Box HM 1070, Hamilton HM-EX (800–343–7170). At press time, the management contract on this, the best of the big-name hotels, was up for reassignment, which could bring management and operational changes. Check for late developments. This luxury resort spent over $13 million in a total restoration and face lift that didn't include the $1 million already spent on a European health spa and fitness center that offers exercise classes from aerobics to dance, Swiss showers, saunas, massage, whirlpool, and full-scale beauty programs. The thick off-white walls, made of Bermuda moonstone, house 700 guests at a time, some 60 percent of whom are repeats. Newly done rooms are in dusty rose, mauve, and pink with light-colored wicker-type furniture. The 25-acre property houses tennis courts with resident pro, swimming on several beaches, heated outdoor pool and a glass-dome-enclosed indoor pool, snorkeling and scuba shop, as well as volleyball, badminton, shuffleboard, water skiing, and windsurfing. Restaurants include the upscale *Lillians,* a popular supper club; the *Port Royal,* with combination American and French dishes; the *Greenhouse,* with nouvelle cuisine touches on an international menu; and a Parisian-style bistro named simply *The Cafe.* Spa packages are well thought out, mixing half-day spa programs with four- to seven-day plans. A highly skilled staff counsels guests individually to help them create a personalized program, and also encourages an at-home health, beauty, and fitness routine. (*MAP; BP; EP*)

*Southampton Princess, Box HM 1379, Hamilton HM-FX (800–223–1818). The other Princess hotel on the island, this one sits atop a 60-acre estate with a commanding view of all Bermuda. Over 1,000 guests flock to this large, self-contained resort and love its international atmosphere. A $20-million renovation of the property reflects the clean, airy charm of the area. There are two shopping arcades, beauty salons, health club, two swimming pools, a private beach club with *Whaler Inn* and *Shipwreck Bar,* 11 tennis courts, fishing and other water sports, an 18-hole executive par-3 golf course, several restaurants, as well as the *Waterlot Inn* down on the other shore, and top-rate entertainment in the *Empire Room,* disco dancing in *The Touch Club,* and a combo in *Neptune Bar* and *Shipwreck Bar* nightly. The *Newport Room* is considered one of Bermuda's best dining experiences, while the three-tiered *Windows on the Sound* has dinner-dancing nightly with orchestra. There are even 100 suites, including a deluxe suite that has three double bedrooms, living room, four baths, and balcony. Views are magnificent from all the balconied rooms. Rates are expensive but honeymoon, tennis, and golf packages are available. (*EP*)

Small Hotels

*Glencoe, Box PG 297, Paget PG-BX (800–468–1500). Owners Reggie and Margot Cooper have lovingly tended this 250-year old main house from the old sailing days for over 30 years. Since the resort itself is surrounded by water, this is still a place for owners and captains of the sleek yachts anchored at Glencoe's shores, and a room-with-a-view is guaranteed, ranging from spectacular to merely splendid. The Paget location is convenient to Hamilton (via the Salt Kettle ferry), but repeat guests don't seem to want to leave the beach, two swimming pools, and sprawling patio, where breakfast, lunch, and dinner are served; there's also a snazzy dining room inside. Dishes are prepared with a flair by Roberta Williams, the only female head chef on the island. In season, there's music nightly at dinner, and a Saturday night dinner dance on the patio with yachts moored off-shore. Off-season, there's a roaring fire, international conversations, and impromptu piano evenings. The property has one of the best windsurfing schools in Bermuda, plus small boat rentals. (*MAP; BP*)

*Hamiltonian Hotel and Island Club, Box HM 1738, Hamilton HM-GX (295–5608). Originally built in 1841 as the private mansion of a local sea captain, this property atop Mt. Langton was formerly Sherwood's Hotel. Now under new ownership and upgraded to more luxury standards, the Hamiltonian is part hotel and part private club for timeshare members. There are accommodations for 150 guests in 43 rooms and 32 suites. The Hamiltonian has one of the largest fresh water pools on the island (solar heated), plus three tennis courts with year-round pro, a beach facility on the North Shore, and complimentary transportation to Horseshoe Beach. Along with panoramic views, the Hamiltonian also has the Bermuda Lounge for evening cocktails, a main dining room, and gourmet restaurant. Near the tennis courts is a small pub for drinks from noon to 10 P.M. (*MAP; BP; EP*)

*Harmony Club, Box PG 299, Paget PG-BX (800–223–5672). Owners Trusthouse Forte have now made this a club aimed at couples only under an all-inclusive staying price. The gardens are among the most beautiful on an island filled with English landscaping and Bermuda blossoms. The 144 guests stay in cottage-type rooms in the main building or in units around the garden. There is a small pool, two tennis courts, a putting green, and shuffleboard on the grounds. Golf can be arranged in Belmont, as can exchange dining. This is the best of both worlds—friendly and small but offering guests the use of the facilities at the larger property. (*MAP; BP; EP*)

*Mermaid Beach Club, Box WK 250, Warwick WK-BX (800–441–7087). As with many Bermuda properties, these housekeeping apartments and hotel got an unintended "refurbishing" due to Emily, the hurricane of 1987, forcing owners to redecorate and update this prime property. Restaurant on premises and meals available at *Miramar.* Pool plus private beach. The nautical *Old Ship Pub* has a guitarist nightly. Modern one- and two-bedroom apartments, suites, and bed/sitting rooms with private balconies and fully equipped kitchens on request. (*MAP*)

Newstead, Box PG 196, Paget PG-BX (800–468–4111). Situated on Harbour Road overlooking Hamilton Harbour, this 50-room hotel began life as a single manor house, but over the years has assimilated nearby properties and houses, the result being that many of the public rooms are pleasant while the guest rooms are less so. On the well-kept grounds are two tennis courts, a pool, sauna, and complimentary tea and cookies each afternoon. Arrangements can be made for ocean swimming, golf, tennis, or lunch, at the luxurious Coral Beach and Tennis Club, a sister property. (*MAP; BP*)

*Palmetto Hotel and Cottages, Box FL 54, Flatt's FX-BX (800–982–0026). Modern guest rooms and cottage units for 84 persons are located on the edge of Harrington Sound and Flatts Village. The main house is another old Bermuda mansion with two comfortable lounges, *Ha'Penny Pub* and *The Inlet,* and terrace overlooking the pool and sound. Good boating and swimming from the dock; tennis, golf, and other water sports can be arranged by the management. Guests can use John Smith's Bay. Golf, health/beauty, and honeymooner special packages are offered. (*MAP; BP*)

Pompano Beach Club, 32 Pompano Beach Road, Southampton SB-03 (800–343–4155). Cottage units for 160 guests are dramatically placed on a hillside overlooking the ocean. Every room with a view! Dining in the main clubhouse overlooking the ocean. Pool and bar on the upper level; down below, a small beach and private dock. Boat for reef fishing and scuba diving leaves from here. There is one clay tennis court for guests and golf can be arranged at nearby Port Royal Golf Course. Informal, casual atmosphere here that has great appeal. Honeymoon, golf, and family special packages. (*MAP; BP; EP*)

The Reefs, 56 South Road, Southampton SN-02 (800–223–1363). A casually elegant cabana colony perched on a cliff overlooking the South Shore and its own private beach. There is room here for over 198 guests, but it seems much smaller and more intimate. The large, secluded beach has a beachside thatched roof restaurant, *Coconuts,* with unbrellaed tables, and the *Sand Bar* deck tucked to one side. Afternoon tea is taken in the main house, with formal dining in the *Clubhouse Dining Room,* or at the no-smoking tables in the new *Conservatory Room,* where you'll find attentive service. There are two new all-weather tennis courts, but it's the heated swimming pool, surrounded by flower and fauna, that's a daytime conversation center; informal dancing in the evening. Sonesta and the Southampton Princess are just up the road for a more active evening out. David and Bonnie Dodwell have been owner-managers for 15 years. This is a special place for repeat guests who often rebook a year in advance. (*MAP; BP*)

Rosedon, Box HM 290, Hamilton HM-AX (800–225–5567). Colonial charm in the main house of this small hotel (85 guests) in Hamilton, across the road from the Princess Hotel. Price of accommodations includes breakfast in your room, on the veranda, or by the pool, but no other meals are served. It's a five-minute walk into town when you can tear yourself away from the lovely grounds. Tennis at Elbow Beach Hotel and other sports can be arranged. Rosedon is the perfect spot for a quiet, do-it-yourself holiday. (*BP*)

Royal Palms Club Hotel & Restaurant, Box HM 499, Hamilton HM-CX (800–982–0026). This is a small hotel, with room for 41 guests in an old Bermuda house, within walking distance of Hamilton. Owners keep expansive gardens well-primed, and the club is known for its first-rate restaurant. (*EP; MAP*)

*Stonington Beach Hotel, Box 523, Hamilton HM-CX (800–223–1588). Located next to the Elbow Beach Hotel, this is both a hotel and a three-year college for aspiring hoteliers—many of whom parlay their classroom studies and real-life experience into berths at top hotels in the U.S. and Canada. The young staff radiates enthusiasm, and although some of the niceties of service are not yet learned, the savvy crowd that stays here is appreciative of the staff's efforts and energy. The hotel, opened in 1980, has 64 balconied rooms, each with floral accents in decorator fabrics and Bermuda prints on the walls. There's a private beach, a terrific restaurant, tennis courts, and full-time professional management to lend continuity to staff operations. Very good value for the money. (*BP*)

Waterloo House, Box HM 333, Hamilton HM-BX (800–468–4100). Conveniently located in Hamilton, this small harborside hotel can accommodate 70 guests, who are given keys to the large cedar street entrance door when they go out in the evening. A short walk to Hamilton and the ferry. A definite plus is the welcome that guests receive at the Coral Beach and Tennis Club, a sister property, for golf, swimming, or lunch. (*MAP; BP*)

White Sands and Cottages, Box PG 196, Paget PG-BX (800–548–0547). Overlooking Grape Bay on the south shore, this small hotel (80 guests) has an informal and casual atmosphere and is just the place for families and honeymooners who do not want organized activity. Cottages are below the main house and Grape Bay Beach is a six-minute walk. Lovely views from outdoor terrace overlooking the sea where weekly swizzle parties and barbecues take place. Special monthly rental for some cottages. (*MAP; BP; EP*)

Cottage Colonies

Ariel Sands Beach Club, Box HM 334, Hamilton HM-BX (800–468–6610). Lovely location along the South Shore. Groups of cottages are situated up and down low-grade hill. There are 11 cottage units with private porches in all. Three all-weather tennis courts plus a large swimming pool with patio and snack bar. Reef-snorkeling equipment is available for rent but *beware* of the reefs. A pleasant and restful place for some 90 guests. One of the guests likes the place so much, she donated a wire statue that plays in the foaming surf. Perfect for couples or families. Informal dancing outdoors, barbecues, and candlelight buffets. Very personable management. (*MAP; BP*)

Cambridge Beaches, 30 King's Point, Sandys MA-02 (800–468–7300). Seventy-five rooms individually decorated. Then there's "Pegem," a 300-year-old cottage where the beams in the cathedral ceilings of Bermudian cedar were put together with wooden pegs. Built by a pirate, his storeroom is now the dining room with an antique dining table for eight. (This particular two-bedroom cottage for four is $850 MAP.) Managing director Michael Winfield seems genuinely in love with his property on a 25-acre peninsula. He knows of "at least" 6 beaches on the property itself, along with inlets of sand and surf. Each cottage has an individual name and decor, with many art works by Bermudian artists. There are 14 different menus for two-weeks' rotation of dining choices. The hotel will also pack picnic baskets for beach picnics. There are sailing trips twice weekly and nightly entertainment from a pianist to a vocal trio. (*MAP*)

*Flamingo Beach Club, Box HM 466, Hamilton HM-BX (800–441–7087). This is a recent amalgamation of the Flamingo Beach Club and Montgomery Cottages with a total capacity for 22 guests. All cottages (except 10 units at Flamingo Beach) have fully equipped kitchens. At Flamingo Beach, cottage units are in a garden setting overlooking the south shore and ocean. Relaxed atmosphere with a variety of accommodations to suit all tastes in a central location. The *Jolly Lobster* serves upper-crust crustaceans! (*EP; BP*)

Horizons, Box PG 198, Paget PG-BX (800–468–0022). A total of 50 rooms, suites, and duplex cottages sprawl across 25 acres, inland of the south shore. French, Swiss, U.K., and German guests head the list, followed by Americans and Canadians. The ambience is carefully and caringly European, with German-born William Sack as ever-present manager. Under Sack's direction, Horizons has been appointed to "Relais et Château" standing—an international distinction in the world of haute cuisine. The individuality of Horizons is especially evident in the main rooms, where the art work of Gill Ingham is on display. Her artistic fabrics, antiques, and antique reproductions can be seen throughout the hotel. The coral-pink main house, which dates from the late 17th century, is a Bermuda landmark. Very special is that an individual cook is assigned to cook each guest's breakfast in his or her cottage, then serve it on a private patio. There are three tennis courts, a nine-hole golf course, swimming pool, and evening entertainment three nights a week. (*MAP*)

Lantana Colony Club, Box SB90, Sandys SB-BX (800–468–3733). The most elegant of all the cottage colonies is also a "museum without walls" exhibiting priceless sculptures and paintings within the hotel and on the grounds. The clubhouse is pure Bermudian and the 100-plus guests live in luxurious cottages around 20-some acres of lush landscaped gardens. All have private porches, kitchenettes for cold breakfast-in-bed, and are equipped with hair dryers and irons. There are two all-weather courts, putting green, croquet lawn, shuffleboard, private dock for water skiing and sunfish, plus large pool and *La Plage* glass-enclosed terrace restaurant. The ferry ride to Hamilton from Somerset Bridge (30 to 45 minutes) is complimentary to guests. But who wants to leave? (*MAP*)

Pink Beach Club, Box HM 1017, Hamilton HM-DX (800–372–1323). Once, this was "the" place to stay in Bermuda, but now the elegance is fading. Still, this is a quiet colony of pink cottages surrounding a private beach along the south shore. This property can accommodate 148 guests. There are 20 acres of landscaped grounds, a main clubhouse, large pool and terrace, two all-weather tennis courts, dancing, and barbecues for the guests. High rates for an exclusive, quiet area that mixes British traditions with Bermuda charm. (*MAP*)

Willowbank, Box MA 296, Sandys MA-BX (234–1616). A simple cottage colony located on Ely's Harbour on the south shore with religious overtones. Morning devotional period is set aside for those who wish to attend. Meals are served family-style in the main dining room. No liquor is served. Accommodations for 114 guests in cottages on seven acres of grounds. There is a swimming pool and one tennis court. Ideal for a quiet family vacation. Low rates. (*MAP*)

Clubs

Coral Beach and Tennis Club, 34 South Road, Paget PG-04 (236–2233). This is a private club and introduction by a member or former guest is required. There are accommodations for 133 guests on a lovely beach property along the south shore. Excellent tennis facilities on seven courts, with a tennis pro and round robin tournaments on Sunday. There are two squash courts, an 18-hole putting green, lawn bowling, and croquet on the premises. Beautiful beach. Guests and members may use the swimming pool and nine-hole mashie golf course at Horizons across the road. Dinner is served in main clubhouse (formal on Thursday and Saturday nights). Informal *Beach Terrace* with bar overlooking the large, private stretch of beach. (*BP*)

Mid-Ocean Club, Box HM 1728, Hamilton HM-GX (293–0330). Introduction by a member is definitely required at this distinguished Bermuda club in fashionable Tucker's Town. A large estate on the edge of the ocean that has played host to statesmen from Britain, France, and the U.S., it has its own private 18-hole championship course plus two all-weather tennis courts. Rates on request, 32 guests only. Members, or their guests, only. Expensive and exclusive.

St. George's Club, Box GE 92, St. George's GE-BX (297–1200). This is a "club" in name only, since guests can pay to play and don't require the international social connections of the hallowed Mid-Ocean Club and upright Coral Beach Club. Situated where the old St. George's Hotel once looked over the quaint town and harbor, this 18-acre property on lease from the government for 55 years is another Bermuda time-share resort with a hotel license as well. Two-bedroom cottages with views and beautiful decor are available on an annual basis for the next 25 years for one payment of $8,000 to $26,000 (depending upon location) plus token maintenance charges. Or, you may book a cottage for about $250 to $450 per day (*EP*). Facilities also include a luxurious clubhouse, Olympic-sized swimming pool, 18-hole golf course designed by Robert Trent Jones, tennis courts, the *Margaret Rose* restaurant, *Sir George Pub,* and beach just minutes away. To buy into St. George's Club means membership in Resort Condominiums International and the right to trade your Bermuda unit for a stay at any of 1,500 member resorts worldwide. The St. George's location is an added plus. Guests should take time to talk to Rebecca Browne in the sales office—she's a valued information source. (*EP*)

Housekeeping Cottages and Apartments (Large)

Astwood Cove, 49 South Road, Warwick WK-07 (236–0984). In a 1710 main house, surrounded by palm, banana, and citrus trees, there are 18 modern suite-apartments for 57 guests on South Shore Road. The building is perched on a hill, with panoramic views of well-tended gardens and the ocean, a short drive or stroll away. Owner Nicky Lewin describes himself as the "manager-bellboy," and his wife Gabrielle, as the hostess-owner. Both add, "there are 18 restaurants within two miles!" Pool, sauna, and convenient to golf courses and south shore beaches. (*EP*)

Clear View Suites, 10 Sandy Lane, North Shore, Hamilton CR-02 (800–468–9600). These units for 24 guests are located on the water's edge off North Shore Road. Fishing, swimming, and snorkeling off private waterfront. Between Flatts Village and St. George's for shopping and entertainment. (*EP*)

Longtail Cliffs, Box HM 836, Hamilton HM-CX (236–2822). Modern housekeeping apartments for 48 guests, overlooking the ocean. All have covered porches and use of a small private beach. Swimming pool and maid service. (*EP*)

Munro Beach Cottages, Box SN 99, Southampton SN-BX (234–1175). Attractive, modern duplex cottage units less than 91 meters (100 yards) from the beach on Whitney Bay, along the south shore. Bordered on three sides by Port Royal Golf Course, with its own extensive grounds. Guest capacity is 32 in secluded area. Excellent for families. (*EP*)

Pretty Penny, Box PG 137, Paget PG-BX (236–1194). A guest house-small hotel with amenities and pizazz. Owner Stephen Martin completely revamped this nine-unit property in 1984. Studios and one bedrooms, all with kitchenettes, and one unit with a fireplace and a cat who has elected to live there. Each room has a definite, distinctive decor. The many repeat guests make their own contributions—one artist has created paintings for "his" room. All guests are personally cared for by Martin and his staff, and are introduced to one another at regular cocktail gatherings. Not inexpensive, but worth it.

Rosemont, Box HM 37, Hamilton HM-AX (800–367–0040). Housekeeping units for 56 guests situated on a hillside overlooking Hamilton Harbour. Just a short walk to town and ferry. Apartments are built on two levels, with penthouse deck and large pool. Children's play area and laundry facilities. Wheelchair guests welcome. (*EP*)

*Sandpiper Guest Apartments, Box HM 685, Hamilton HM-CX (236–7093). Modern and spacious apartments with nine efficiency units on South Road. Close to beaches. Small garden and swimming pool. (*EP*)

*Sky Top, Box PG 227, Paget PG-BX (236–7984). Location (opposite Elbow Beach), view (atop a coral cliff), and price ($65 to $95 for two, in season), are right. There's a total of 11 units, ranging from studios to one-bedroom, basic in decor, but clean and cheery. Owners Marion Stubbs and Susan Harvey are usually on the premises to answer questions. While there's no restaurant on the property, there are kitchenettes, and several snacking or dining choices are within walking distance. (*EP*)

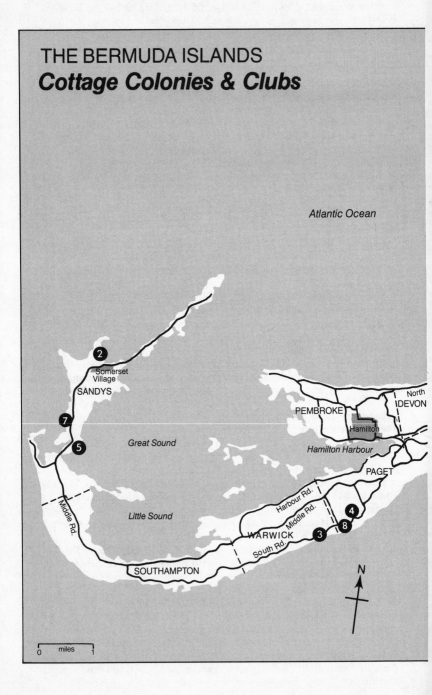

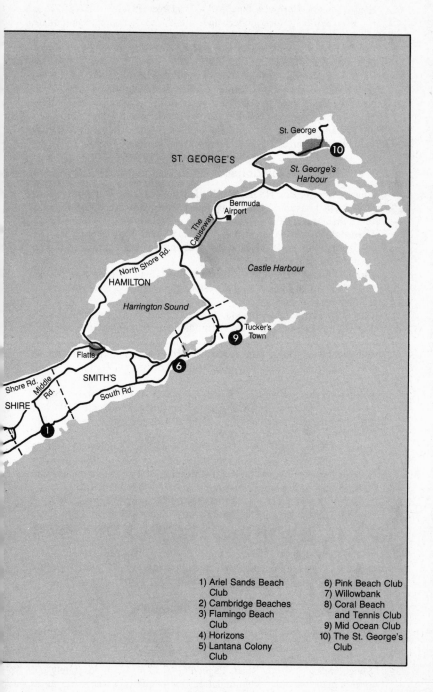

1) Ariel Sands Beach Club
2) Cambridge Beaches
3) Flamingo Beach Club
4) Horizons
5) Lantana Colony Club
6) Pink Beach Club
7) Willowbank
8) Coral Beach and Tennis Club
9) Mid Ocean Club
10) The St. George's Club

South Capers Cottages, Box PG 273, Paget PG-BX (236–1222 or 236–1987). Self-contained modern apartments and cottages accommodate 46 guests and overlook the ocean on the south shore. There are two private pools and it's a three-minute walk to Grape Bay Beach. Perfect for families with children (laundry facilities). (*EP*)

Surf Side Beach Club, Box WK 101, Warwick WX-BX (800–553–9990). A varied group of cottages and apartments overlook the south shore from landscaped, terraced levels. Beautiful pool (one for children, too) as well as a private beach. Large sun terrace and coffee shop open from 8:30 A.M. to 3 P.M. Accommodations for 74 guests in lovely location, which owner-manager Bryony Harvey keeps in top condition. (*EP*)

Housekeeping Cottages and Apartments (Small)

Angel's Grotto, Box HS 62, Smith's HS-BX (295–6437). Property consists of main house and cottage complex. One- and two-bedroom units with kitchenettes. (*EP*)

Barnsdale Guest Apartments, Box DV 628, Devonshire DV-BX (236–0164). Four small efficiency apartments in residential area. Small garden. (*EP*)

Burch's Guest House, 110 North Shore Road, Devonshire FL-03 (292–5746). Room for 20 guests overlooking north shore. Small garden, close to bus stop. (*EP*)

Cabana Vacation Apartments, 61 Verdmont Road, Smith's FL-BX (296–6964). A two-centuries-old Bermuda house redesigned into comfortable, self-contained apartments, each with private entrance. Cedar-beamed clubroom, large pool in garden setting. Accommodations for 16 guests in informal and friendly atmosphere. Located on Verdmont Road. (*EP*)

Garden House, 4 Middle Road, Somerset Bridge, Sandys SB-01 (234–1435). Located at Somerset Bridge and managed by Rosie Galloway, Garden House accommodates 12 persons in cottages for two or four. (*BP; EP*)

Robin's Nest, 10 Vale Close, North Shore, Pembroke HM-04 (292–4347). Housekeeping units for 12 in secluded residential area, with attractive gardens. Private, informal atmosphere. About a five-minute ride to Hamilton for shopping, restaurants, and entertainment. (*EP*)

Syl-Den Apartments, 8 Warwickshire Road, Warwick WK-02 (238–1834). Housekeeping apartments for 10 guests close to south shore beaches. Informal atmosphere in residential area of Warwickshire Estate, off South Road. (*EP*)

Valley Cottages, Box PG 214, Paget PG-BX (236–0628). Informal old Bermuda cottages and self-contained apartments for 23 guests opening onto garden setting. Near Elbow Beach and supermarket. (*EP*)

Guest Houses (Large)

Archlyn Villa, Box HM 220, Hamilton HM-AX (292–1405). Informal accommodations for 24 guests overlooking Mill's Creek and Fairylands. Large lounge and solarium, spacious garden. (*CP; EP*)

Loughlands, 79 South Road, Paget PG-03 (236–1253). A stately old Bermuda mansion with accommodations for 43 guests. Extensive grounds and gardens. Family-style lounge and dining room. Convenient to beaches, golf, and entertainment. (*CP*)

Woodbourne/Inverness, Box HM 977, Hamilton HM-DX (295–3737). Two guest houses with total accommodations for 28 guests. Within walking distance of Hamilton and ferry. Comfortable and informal. (*CP*)

Guest Houses (Small)

Edgehill Manor, Box HM 1048, Hamilton HM-EX (295–7124). Outskirts of Hamilton, with accommodations for 18. Pool and patio in garden area. (*CP*)

Fordham Hall, Box HM 692, Hamilton 5 (800–537–4163). Rooms for 20 guests with large lounge downstairs, sitting room with harbor view upstairs. Within walking distance of Hamilton shops and ferry. (*CP*)

Serenity, Box PG 34, Paget 6 (296–7419). Quiet guest house on St. Michael's Road with large bedrooms and small garden. Accommodates six guests. (*BP; EP*)

Hillcrest Guest House, Box GE 96, St. George GE-BX (297–1630). Old Bermuda home with large veranda and views of St. George Harbour. In historic area. Accommodations for 19 guests. Large garden and spacious lawns. (*EP*)

Hi-Roy, 22 Princess Estate Road, Pembroke HM-04 (292–0808). Small, modern guest house in Princess Estates off North Shore Road. Large lounge, home-cooked meals for 13 guests. (*MAP; BP*)

Little Pomander, 16 Pomander Road, Paget HM-BX (236–7635). Located on edge of Hamilton Harbour. Casual atmosphere for 16 guests. Old Bermuda cottage with waterfront garden patio and barbecue. (*CP*)

Royal Heights, Box SN 144, Southampton SN-BX (238–0043). Bedrooms with terraces for 15 guests. Swimming pool and comfortable lounge with views of the Great Sound. Informal accommodations on Lighthouse Hill. (*BP*)

Salt Kettle House, 10 Salt Kettle Road, Paget PG-01 (236–0407). Rooms, cottages, and apartments for 22 guests in garden setting. Small cove and dock on harbor inlet with swimming. One of Bermuda's best locations and a favorite with visitors. (*BP*)

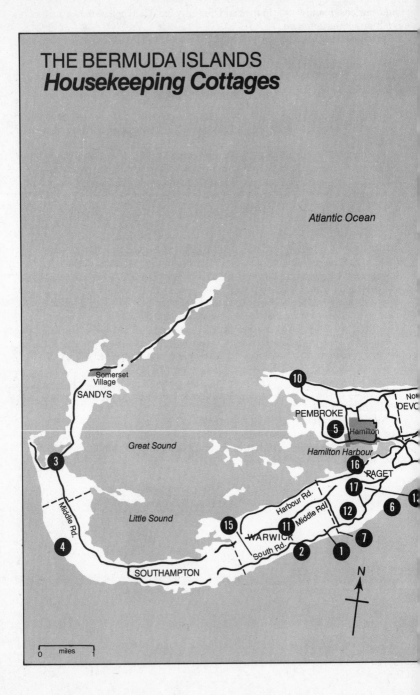

THE BERMUDA ISLANDS
Housekeeping Cottages

Atlantic Ocean

Somerset
Village
SANDYS

PEMBROKE

Hamilton

Great Sound

Hamilton Harbour

PAGET

Middle Rd.

Little Sound

Harbour Rd.

Middle Rd.

WARWICK

South Rd.

SOUTHAMPTON

N

miles
0   1

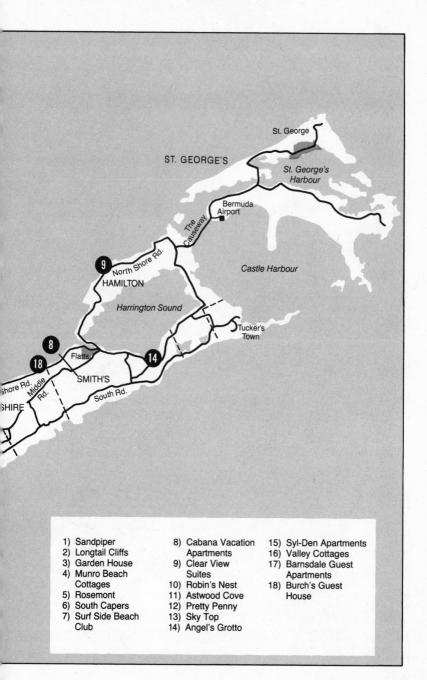

1) Sandpiper
2) Longtail Cliffs
3) Garden House
4) Munro Beach Cottages
5) Rosemont
6) South Capers
7) Surf Side Beach Club
8) Cabana Vacation Apartments
9) Clear View Suites
10) Robin's Nest
11) Astwood Cove
12) Pretty Penny
13) Sky Top
14) Angel's Grotto
15) Syl-Den Apartments
16) Valley Cottages
17) Barnsdale Guest Apartments
18) Burch's Guest House

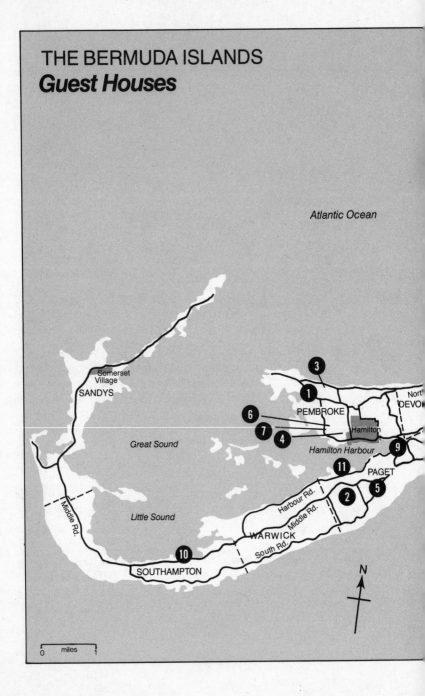

THE BERMUDA ISLANDS
Guest Houses

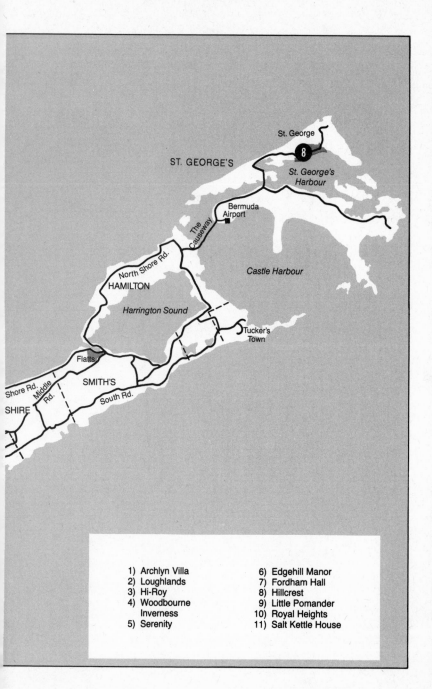

1) Archlyn Villa
2) Loughlands
3) Hi-Roy
4) Woodbourne Inverness
5) Serenity
6) Edgehill Manor
7) Fordham Hall
8) Hillcrest
9) Little Pomander
10) Royal Heights
11) Salt Kettle House

DINING, WINING, AND ENTERTAINMENT

By Candlelight or Alfresco

The end of a perfect day in Bermuda means dining on a lovely terrace under a twinkling sky or indoors with candlelight bouncing across century-old cedar beams. It also means a short motorbike ride to a popular spot to try the local specialties. The island is full of restaurants that serve traditional Bermudian dishes, English and Continental cuisine, or finger food like hamburgers and french fries. But be mindful that food is not a strong point on this island. There are a few—very few—terrific restaurants on an international dining scale: the *Newport Room, Romanoff's,* and all the dining rooms at the cottage colonies are splendid in ambience. Less formal and moderately priced are two excellent, ethnic restaurants in Hamilton, *Chopsticks* and the *Bombay Bicycle Club.*

Traditional Bermudian fare features the many varieties of fish found in the surrounding sea, plus local fruits and vegetables. Many of the recipes have been handed down among families for generations. Indeed, the favorite Christmastime dish of cassava pie is said to be a 300-year-old tradition. It is a meat pie with dough flavored by the cassava root. No good Bermudian home goes without its appearance right next to the very-English plum pudding at holiday time. Another time-honored island custom is Sunday breakfast with a menu of salt cod and bananas. This fruit is one of the local staples and Bermudians bake them, fry them, fritter them, and use

121

them in puddings and bread. The sweet Bermuda onion is another local favorite and popular dishes are onion pie, cheese and onion sandwiches, even onions glazed in sugar and rum.

Fish, the major source of nourishment for the early colonists, is creatively used in a number of local specialties. The most famous, of course, is fish chowder, which is served laced with as much black rum and as many sherry peppers as you like. (Sherry peppers are simply made by marinating hot, spicy peppers in sherry for several weeks. Replenish sherry as you use and let "mull" some more.) Restaurant menus also feature Bermuda rock fish, (a firm-fleshed, white fish found in various dishes), red snapper (with onions and potatoes), mussel pie, mussel fritters, Bermuda shark, and succulent Bermuda spiny lobster (in season from the first of September through March). Hoppin' John and Bermuda syllabub are two other dishes that should not be overlooked. The former is a mixture of rice, peas, onions, bacon, thyme, and chicken and served as a main course. The latter is a dessert that combines guava jelly, wine, and cream. Delicious!

If you wish to dine at the more elegant and expensive restaurants on the island, it is best to book ahead and check on the dress requirements. Many restaurants, especially in hotels, request that gentlemen wear jacket and tie and that their companions are also appropriately garbed. Dinner prices in these restaurants compare to those in other resorts and can run over $100 per person, depending upon the number of courses chosen and types of drinks and wine. Expect a 15-percent service charge.

Many of the larger restaurants (with the exception of those in hotels and cottage colonies) will accept credit cards, mainly *American Express,* but *MasterCard* and *Visa* are also accepted at most. If you do not wish to pay cash, check credit information when you call to book a table.

The price categories we use are approximations for an average three-course meal per person. They do not include wine, drinks, or gratuities. **Expensive and Elegant** and **Expensive Specialty** restaurants will cost $35 to $45 for lunch, and $50 and up for dinner. **Moderate** restaurants will cost $20 to $30 for lunch, and $30 and up for dinner. **Very Affordable** meals will cost $10 to $15 for lunch, and $15 to $30 for dinner.

RESTAURANTS

Elegant and Expensive

Fourways Inn, Paget. At the very top of fine dining in Bermuda, this gourmet restaurant is in an 18th-century Georgian home full of highly polished cedar beams and balustrades. It is a culinary adventure and, indeed, your meal will be remembered long after you have paid the bill. The menu is impressive and specialties include fresh mussels simmered in white wine and cream, fresh veal sautéed in lemon butter, Caesar salad, and strawberry soufflé. But every dish here is a specialty and served with a flourish. Carafe wine is available, as are all other drinks—the Fourways Special combines loquat liqueur with juices and bitters. There is an excellent wine list. Open seven days a week for lunch and dinner (brunch now served daily, with gourmet brunch on Thursdays and Sundays) and dining is outside in season. All credit cards; gratuities added to the bill. (236–6517)

Henry VIII Pub-Restaurant, Southampton Parish. This has become a Bermuda tradition—a very tourist-oriented one—in Tudor surroundings with service by young ladies dressed as "wenches." There are wooden tables and chairs and diamond-paned windows that open up in the summer. The restaurant is located at the top of the hill, overlooking Sonesta Beach Hotel and the south shore. Local Bermudian and English fare features beef, juicy lamb, mussel pie, steak and kidney pie, and seafood casseroles. Wonderful onion soup, turtle soup, and hearty King and Queen salads. Lunch noon to 2:30 P.M.; sandwiches 2:30 to 4 P.M.; dinner 7 to 10:30 P.M. Sunday brunch from noon to 3 P.M. Entertainment nightly in Henry's Pub and sing-alongs after 11 P.M. Also King's Pantry and Liquor Store adjacent, with wines, spirits, cold beer, and snacks for the beach. (238–1977 or 238–0908)

Newport Room, Southampton Princess. One of Bermuda's finest restaurants, the Newport Room is named and themed after that pinnacle of yacht-racing silver, the America's Cup. At this most formal of restaurants, there are cases with models of previous America's Cup winners arrayed on a solid teak floor and surrounded by teak walls. Gerard Vie of France has organized the menu with Guy Maresse into a cuisine moderne. Although the menu changes every three months, a few favorites remain: *tapenade,* a fresh fish with black olive sauce, from the south of France; Chef Vie's recipe for fresh salmon cooked on one side only, with dill; a veal chop with lobster sauce and langoustines; an imported sirloin steak with béarnaise sauce. There is also a "menu degustation" that allows the tasting of a small portion of many dishes from the à la carte menu. (238–8167).

Romanoff's, Church Street, Hamilton. Owner-maitre d', Antun Duzavic, proudly offers a distinctive toast to each guest: ice cold Russian vodka and a bite of caviar! After that, it might be his award-winning specialty, Tournedos flambe Alexandra, or steak tartare. There's also a sprinkling of Russian dishes: shashlyk Georgian style; sole Douvres Walewska (poached Dover sole in a lobster and shrimp sauce); filet of beef Stroganoff; or perhaps, stuffed filet of sole with salmon mousse in champagne. Ask Duzavic about his very special "specials" that aren't on the menu. (295–0333)

Tivoli Gardens, Reid Street, Hamilton. Housed in the restored old Hamilton Armoury, this restaurant features a Danish menu in Bermudian landmark surroundings. Local cedar ceiling beams and shutters, large bronze chandeliers, and lots of foliage throughout. Open daily from noon to 2:30 P.M. and 6 to 10 P.M. (295–8592).

Tom Moore's Tavern, Bailey's Bay, Hamilton Parish. This restaurant certainly made a splash when it was reopened in 1986 by restaurateur Franco Bortoli. It's a beautiful setting, with fireplaces, casement windows, stucco white walls and copper appointments. But the instant success may need the tempering of time. Diners are well-dressed island visitors (not Bermudians, who seem to dine elsewhere). The boned crisp duckling roasted with natural juice and a touch of rosemary vinegar had been roasted a bit too long, but the baked salmon was excellent. One of the more intriguing dishes is, "Treasures of Saint David's Island," Bermuda fish, flame fish, and lobster tail. The chef's specialty is quail filled with goose liver and morels, truffled and baked in puff pastry. Good to inconsistent. (293–8020)

Waterlot Inn, Middle Road, Southampton. Housed by the Southampton Princess, this restaurant dates from 1670. Famous people who have sipped and supped here include Eleanor Roosevelt, James Thurber, and

Eugene O'Neill. That's the good news. The bad news is that this once-special spot has slipped—badly. The staff is surly, and the food is indifferent. The view can be splendid, so we suggest a drink, if the inn is on your must-visit list. (238–0510)

Expensive Specialty Restaurants

Carriage House, Somers Wharf, St. George's. This is part of the Somers Wharf restoration, geared for a heavy turnover in the stopping and cruise ship clientele. The dinner dishes are hearty and good, from English spring lamb to prime ribs cut from a trolly. The best bet, however, is a reasonable Sunday brunch (about $17 per person), that offers nonstop wine, along with a plentiful buffet of eggs, pancakes, meats, fresh fish, pasta, salads, veggies, and desserts galore. (297–1270 or 297–1730)

Horizons, Paget. The chef is English, there's a German-Swiss at the cold buffet table, an Austrian in the soup and, of course, the pastry is French. Limited outside reservations accepted for a $37 prix fixe dinner (plus 15% service charge). The restaurant grows many of its own vegetables, and there are 70 wines on the list, some as unusual as Swiss Fondant and pink champagne. (236–0048)

Little Venice, Bermudiana Road, Hamilton. This is a very "in" spot for lunch with local executives, and it does help to be a known name (reservations a must). The menu has more of a sense of humor than does the maitre d': *penne Gorbachev* is worthy of its name—pasta tossed with salmon, then flamed in vodka, with cream and tomatoes. Split a Caesar salad for a starter and pay special attention to the thin slices of bread baked in a garlic and herb sauce. At night, there's complimentary admission to the Club upstairs (there's an $8 admission charge for others). (295–3503)

Penthouse, town of Hamilton. Right on Front Street, upstairs from the Longtail Bar, this is an old favorite among the local residents and is among the nicer restaurants on the island. Continental menu in a classy decor. Both Bermuda fish and beef are featured in a variety of *haute cuisine* methods, while appetizers and desserts are strictly gourmet. End the meal with Crêpes au Grand Marnier and enjoy the flames! Ask for the window overlooking the harbor. Lunch (Monday through Friday) from 12 noon; and dinner (Monday through Saturday) from 7 P.M. (292–3414)

Plantation, Bailey's Bay, Hamilton. A club atmosphere prevails here, particularly at dinner, where intimate chatter fills the wicker-decorated dining room, which merges with a glassed-in atrium complete with plants and flickering candles. The food is predominantly from the sea—mahimahi; monkfish poached and served with pineapple, raisins, coconuts, mango, and curry; pan-fried fish with prawns and coconuts. There's a showing of meat dishes; pork trinity and lamb loquat; also, filet mignon. (293–1188)

Rum Runners, city of Hamilton. This restaurant on Front Street has a nautical decor and boasts two patios (one overlooking Hamilton Harbour), three indoor dining rooms, and two pub-style bars. A la carte dining in the main room in the evening is formal (jacket and tie required) but casual during the day and in the other areas at night. Menu is American, English, and European, with Bermuda lobster in season and fresh seafood a specialty. Lunch and dinner. Extensive salad bar in *Lord Halifax Dining Room* at lunch Monday–Friday. (292–4737)

Tavern on the Green, Botanical Gardens. Different menu and decor here now, with increased seating for over 100. Open daily for lunch and dinner, with small dance floor and secluded "honeymoon" section. The Roman decor includes a statue of Caesar himself and a waterfall; all diners have good views of the garden. Eight-page menu features French/Italian dishes in the Mediterranean style and a choice of some 60 different wines. Kitchen staffed by four European chefs. This restaurant competes with the best on the island. Two brunch menus available on Sundays, for served meals with complimentary champagne. (295–7731 or 295–9620)

Whaler Inn, Southampton Princess Beach Club. Wahoo, yellowfin tuna, dolphin, barracuda, shark, and Bermuda fish, all "swim" through the menu. Intriguing combinations go into a kettle of seafood St. David's, with clams, mussels, lobster, Bermuda fish, scallops, and shrimps, all poached in fish stock. (Note: Closed December to March.) Sunday brunch is very popular. (238–0076)

Moderate Restaurants

Black Horse Tavern, St. David's Island. Strictly a Bermudian crowd around the six outside picnic tables or the inside clean and casual dining room with circular fans and plants. Owner Gary Lamb is out every morning catching the conch that turns into curried conch stew with rice; the mussels, also served with rice; and the shark hash. His specialties are pan-fried filet of fish that could be amber, rockfish, shark, tuna, or wahoo— and, in season, broiled Bermuda lobster. Be sure to add a dash of their own hot sauce, homemade by chef Bernel Pitcher. This is one of the few feeding spots that stays open all day; 11 A.M. to 1 A.M. (293–9742)

Bombay Bicycle Club, Reid Street, Hamilton. This hot—literally and figuratively—spot for lunch and dinner took the town by storm when it opened with a menu of 55 entrees. Not only is Chef Singh a native of India, all his kitchen staff are countrymen as well (the owner is English-Bermudian). The decor is true to the days of the Raj: dark woods, ceiling fans, and rich, soft sofas in the secluded bar, and heavy wicker chairs at the formally draped tables. Here, spices are used both sparingly and generously, as true Indian cuisine requires: 12 tandoor dishes from a proper tandoori oven; fresh Bermuda fish, in a *masala* or *amritsari* sauce; lamb *roganjosh, saagwala, biryani,* or *achar-e-gosht* (this one is *hot!*). New Continental dishes are currently being added. An offbeat spot that's fun and frequented by locals, it gets high marks for achievement. (292–0048)

Botanic Garden Tea Room, town of Hamilton. Located in Trimingham's, this is a favored spot for a shopping stop. Lunch and tea served from 11:30 A.M. to 3 P.M. Open sandwiches, homemade soups, cakes, pastries, yogurt, and fruit salads. Managed by Fourways Inn, so you know it's first-rate. Many different types of tea, coffee, and mineral water to drink. No credit cards. (295–1183)

Chez Lafitte, Reid Street, Hamilton. A second-storey dining room, with the atmosphere of a dark drawing room, that opened to decidedly mixed reviews. The Cajun menu is interesting, however: catfish à la Cajun, Creole Jambalaya, blackened redfish, shark hash, shrimp Creole. (295–0572)

Chopsticks, Reid Street East, Hamilton. Another hit for Bermudian owners who had the savvy to insist on a chef to match the ethnic cuisine. In this case it's Chef Luk, who has a way with a menu that mixes Szechuan, Hunan, and Cantonese dishes. His culinary creations include scallops and asparagus; Mandarin butterfly steak; lemon chicken or chicken Macau; boneless roasted duck; ribs in a Mandarin orange sauce. For dessert, try the fresh-baked "Betty's pies," hot and tempting. (292–0791)

Fisherman's Reef, Burnaby Hill, Hamilton. The nautical decor is an accurate forecast of the menu, which is strongly seafood—Bermuda rockfish, spiny lobster, giant wahoo, tuna, and marlin. But there are also steaks and chops, and a unique "Bermuda Triangle" (scampi, shrimps, steak). (292–1609)

Hog Penny Pub, Burnaby Street, Hamilton. A British pub with paneled rooms, draught beer. Offers prime ribs, fish 'n' chips, calf's liver, wiener schnitzel, chicken Tandoori, fish (fried, frittered, and curried). Lunch and dinner and live entertainment nightly, except Sunday, when closed. (292–2534)

Il Palio, Main Road, Somerset. Italian through and through—there's even pizza, which is possibly the best choice. There's a downstairs bar and second-storey dining room reached by a ship's spiral staircase. A choice of eight antipastos and nine pastas to start, followed by veal, chicken, or beef. (234–1049 or 234–2323)

The Inlet, Palmetto Hotel, Flatts Village. In the winter season this room with a view of the inlet offers stuffed Bermuda lobster, a specialty. Others are rack of lamb and steaks, sizzled and sauced. (293–2323)

Lobster Pot, Bermudiana Road, Hamilton. This is very good seafood at reasonable prices, with a friendly staff serving. The Maine lobster in the holding tank in the foyer could be dinner. Or choose Bermuda fish, stuffed and baked (and that could be rockfish, hind, yellowtail, or snapper). (292–6898)

Loquats, Front Street, Hamilton. Named for the small, plumlike, yellow fruit that ripens in late winter and early spring, this pub/restaurant is one of the newer kids in Hamilton. At lunchtime, the green and white banquettes are likely to be filled with businesswomen and businessmen (in their Bermuda shorts). There are local specialties such as bite-size shark fritters with tarragon mayonnaise, homemade soups, salads that range from Mediterranean-influenced to a chef's salad (that here means Bermuda lobster, shrimps, and slices of roast beef). A local entertainer sings and plays from 9 P.M. until 1 A.M., but this is not their strong point. Open from 11:30 A.M. to 1 A.M. (292–4507)

Loyalty Inn, Sandys Parish. An unpretentious place, this one is a 250-year-old Bermuda home just five minutes' walk from the Watford Bridge ferry landing. Caters to visitors and locals in the Somerset area for luncheon snacks, afternoon drinks, and dinner. Seafood is the backbone of the à la carte menu. (234–0125)

M.R. Onions, Par-la-ville Road, Hamilton. Owner Brian Hetzel took the humble onion—humble anywhere but in Bermuda, where it's a time-honored symbol—and built a very "in" lunch and dinner spot around it. There's onion soup, thick and creamy with croutons and baked cheese, onion brick (bread) on every table, onion quiche and onion burgers, and crisp spinach or chef's salads, as well as standard steaks and chickens. And of course, the Bermuda fish that's on *every* Bermuda restaurant menu. Entertainment at night. (292–5012 or 292–3815)

New Harbourfront, Front Street, Hamilton. An ambitious menu that ranges from guinea chicks (in season), lamb chops in an orange and sherry sauce with scallions, to steak tournedos rolled around paté and prosciutto in a cognac sauce; to salads, soups, and sandwiches. Added value to a full evening is the complimentary admission to the nearby "Club" for 10 P.M. to 3 A.M. disco dancing. (295–4207)

Once Upon a Table, 49 Serpentine Road, Hamilton. The regular menu is memorable, as is the elegant service in this former 18th-century home. Standards are rack of lamb, roast duckling in natural sauce, and pork dashed with whisky. But, given 48 hours notice, the management will prepare a dinner of Bermuda specialties. Open nightly. (295–8585)

Port Royal Golf Course, Southampton Parish. This handsome restaurant overlooks the sea and the 18th hole of the championship Robert Trent Jones-designed government golf course. Golfers are most welcome for steak sandwiches and English beer after the game, but complete meals are also served. Open for breakfast from 8:30 A.M., lunch from 11 A.M. to 3 P.M., and snacks until dusk. Dress is very casual (but no spikes, please). (234–0236)

Primavera, city of Hamilton. A classical Italian menu, with all the veal, pollo, and seafood that a classic selection implies. Rich coffees, espresso, and cappuccino, and even richer desserts. Open for lunch and dinner. (295–2167)

Pub on the Square, St. George's. Smack on King's Square in the middle of historic town of St. George, this British-type pub offers cool draft beer after a morning of sightseeing, juicy hamburgers, or fish and chips. Reasonable and nothing fancy. (297–1522)

The Red Carpet, The Armoury Bldg., 37 Reid Street, Hamilton. The four men in charge here are direct from Italy. The talented chef turns out a number of specialties: homemade pasta (including a ravioli named for Frank Sinatra), veal, fresh fish, beef Stroganoff, and chicken Normand. Small, with lots of brass and mirrors, this place is the spot for lunch in Hamilton—although it's open for dinner, too. (292–6195)

Show Bizz, at the corners of King and Reid Streets, Hamilton. A casual piano bar that serves the best crab cakes in town! Thursday through Saturday, it's alive with Bermudians munching and digging the live entertainment of Wayne Davis, a local pianist and singer. Besides the crab cake munchies, there's Bermuda lobster, chicken teriyaki, lasagne, fettuccine, and basic burgers. Good food, good fun. (292–0676)

Somerset Country Squire, Mangrove Bay, Somerset. An English-style tavern overlooking Mangrove Bay that serves "heaping and hearty," from the steak and kidney pie and curried mussel pie, to bangers and mash. Desserts are dangerous, especially the hot apple pie with whipped cream! (234–0105)

Swizzle Inn, Hamilton Parish. Even the name is marvelous—and home of the famous rum swizzle that has successfully found its way around the entire island. Located just west of the airport, near the Bermuda Perfume Factory and cave area, this is a popular place to stop while touring. Sit outside in good weather and watch the other motorbikes whiz by. Have a swizzle and a game of darts while you wait for your "swizzleburger" to come. (293–0091)

White Horse Tavern, St. George's. Facing King's Square and the harbor, this old tavern with a wide veranda is located on the edge of the bridge to Ordnance Island. Breakfast menu until noon. The location is terrific, but the food is ordinary and the service is aloof. Still, it's a relaxing place to sit, calm hunger pains, and watch the world go by. (297–1838)

Very Affordable

Blue Foam, Somerset Bridge Hotel, Somerset. A small, special restaurant tucked away on Elys Harbour, with a view of small fishing boats and rowboats. Owner Walter Roberts (who is also a member of Parliament) has expanded his nautical-accented dining room to accommodate about 40 patrons. He serves only fresh seafood—from the hard-to-get rockfish to wahoo, dolphin, and langouste; and imported steaks; seafood brochette. Chef Michael Scott has cooked in international competitions and he brought home a gold medal from Japan in the mid-1980s. Open for breakfast, lunch, and dinner. (234–1042)

The Conch Shell, Emporium Bldg., Front Street, Hamilton. Interesting cuisine served on a terrace above the hustle of shoppers below. There's also a pleasant indoor dining room. French and Asian dishes head the menu: slices of veal sautéed in a butter, lemon, and orange sauce; poached filet of Bermuda fish with a ginger cream sauce; fried abalone with oyster sauce; shrimp teriyaki. (295–6969)

Dennis' Hideaway, Cashew City Road on St. David's Island. Owner Dennis Lambe knows a good thing when he's got one going, and there are no plans for improvements. That means there will still be some half-dozen picnic tables on an earth floor for dining, and an immense Bermudian flag waving over the heads of locals, yapping dogs, and drop-in guests studying a chalkboard menu which reads: fish; shrimp; scallops; shark; turtle; stews; conk; mussell; hash of shark; conk fritters; coffee and tea; ice cream. Accessible by land or sea. Not as cheap as you might think, and bring your mosquito repellant! No telephone.

Docksider, Front Street, Hamilton. An in-town pub popular with young people, mostly for the 20 varieties of draft beer from Europe offered at $10.50 a pitcher. The fare is burgers, fish n' chips, and club sandwiches, all nicely presented and downright cheap. (292–4088)

Gunpowder Cavern, Government Hill, St. George's. One of Bermuda's newer restaurants is located in one of the island's oldest forts. Named for William IV (the sailor king) but originally thought to be called Warwick Fort, this structure was dug by hand from the hillside. It was completely rebuilt in 1887 to house gunpowder and other important material needed for the British Atlantic fleet. Inside the fort are folksy bars and a restaurant with Bermuda dishes, British fish 'n' chips, and stateside burgers. The truly food conscious may come for coffee and dessert, rather than the basic menu. Open: 10 A.M. to 1 A.M. daily. (297–0904)

Herman's Restaurant, South Shore Road, Warwick. A simple place but a local favorite, with the same ownership as Show Biz in Hamilton. There's curried lamb or chicken, barbecued chicken and ribs, deep-fried shrimp or scallops, curried mussels, and sweet-and-sour chicken or fish. (298–9635 or 296–7459)

J. Ellsworth, Reid Street, Hamilton. Unpretentious—a place where fish and chips tastes like fish and chips. Could that be because manager-chef Francis Knight does the cooking, and his family has been cooking fish and chips (and other English fare) since 1909? At the advanced age of 25, Knight is a third-generation English cook. It's a proper workingman's menu for snacking at clean wooden tables or take-out: sausage, chicken, fish, all with chips; beef pie or chicken pie; fish sandwiches. The restaurant is named for owner John Ellsworth Roach. (295–1912)

La Trattoria, Washington (between Reid and Church Streets). A most popular dining spot for Italian dishes at affordable prices. Seventeen pizzas are on parade, including a "diet pizza!" There's also pizza Pekinese (sweet 'n' sour sauce) and pizza a la Tzar (with salmon and caviar). Eighteen pasta dishes plus veal, fish, and meat specialties are prepared daily for lunch and dinner. (295–9499 or 295–7059)

Portofino, Bermudiana Road, Hamilton. This casual eatery specializes in pizza (13 kinds), pastas (10 choices), and homemade lasagne and cannelloni. But it's the pizza that has made it a local favorite. Now licensed for liquor, its open daily 11:30 A.M. to 1 A.M. (292–2375 or 295–6090)

Prego, city of Hamilton. Pizza ("Hawaii" to "Vesuvio"); pasta (carbonara to cartoccio); pesce (almondino tomugnaia). This restaurant makes you an offer you shouldn't refuse . . . honest Italian food at low prices. Open for lunch and dinner. (292–1279)

Speciality Inn, Collectors Hill, South Shore. This is a down-home restaurant that's cheerful, clean, and cheap. A drop-in kind of place on the road between Hamilton and St. George's, it offers pasta, seven kinds of pizza, steak, calf's liver, baked and spiced ham, and shakes and ice cream, as well. Soups (fish chowder or red bean) are homemade and piping hot. (236–3133)

Wharf Tavern, Somers Wharf, St. George's. This established restaurant changed hands, menu, and atmosphere last year and now has a more casual look. Chowders are still thick and homemade (Bermuda fish chowder, St. David's conch chowder, Portuguese red bean). There's a proliferation of pizza, basic sandwiches (from ham and cheese to a "wharf" hamburger), and minute steaks. Main courses mix British traditions (steak and kidney pie, shepherd's pie, bangers and mash) with American standards (a 6-ounce steak, barbecued chicken or ribs). (297–1515)

HOTEL AND COTTAGE-COLONY RESTAURANTS

In addition to the many restaurants already mentioned, all of the large hotels and some of the small and the cottage colonies welcome visitors for dinner and evening entertainment. If you are not in accommodations where breakfast and dinner are part of your plan, it is fun to hotel-hop. In fact, it's a good way to educate yourself on what the other properties have to offer. They all have a style of their own, and you will enjoy getting to know them. It is essential to call ahead as restaurants may be fully booked (especially during popular long weekends). Prices can range from moderate to very expensive, but are generally on the expensive side. Be sure to check on dress requirements. As a general rule, gentlemen are expected to appear in jacket and tie and ladies will feel most comfortable in dressy evening wear (take a wrap for air conditioning). As hotel restaurants are fairly expensive, credit cards are usually honored. But check in advance to be sure. Dinner hours also vary as many properties have two sittings. During the summer months, many of these properties also offer a popular outdoor barbecue, with dancing under the stars and some sort of local entertainment. It is a set menu and price, plus service charge and drinks.

City of Hamilton, Pembroke Parish

Waterloo House. This little harborside hotel on the edge of Hamilton has a small, friendly, and very Bermudian dining room. The hotel is associated with Coral Beach, Horizons, and Newstead. (295–4480)

Hamilton Parish

Marriott's Castle Harbour Resort, Tucker's Town. Fun and futuristic best describes *Mikado,* the Japanese steak house located here. In typical Japanese style, the restaurant is designed with black lacquer furnishings, bridges over lily ponds complemented by *shoji* screens, and magnificent art renderings of ceremonial robes. Mikado features a sushi bar and teppanyaki served at the tables or in the intimate Tatami Room. Adjoining the restaurant is the attractive *Blossoms* lounge, a tempting setting for after-dinner drinks and dancing. (293–2040)

Grotto Bay Beach Hotel. Down the road a bit from Castle Harbour near Tucker's Town, Grotto Bay has a pleasant dining room that is famous for its buffets, as well as *Moongate Terrace Restaurant* for lunch and dinner. *Prospero's Cave* disco in an honest-to-goodness cave is on the property. (293–8333)

Smith's Parish

Palmetto Hotel. This small hotel and cottage community on the edge of Harrington Sound and Flatts Village has *The Inlet* restaurant and a terrace for outdoor barbecues. Lively English pub called *Ha'Penny Bar.* (293–2323)

Pink Beach Club and Cottages. An exclusive and luxurious cottage colony with pink cottages surrounding its own private south shore beach. Definitely worth a visit to the landscaped grounds and gardens, dining room, and outdoor barbecues on the terrace. (293–1666)

Devonshire Parish

Ariel Sands. A pleasant cottage colony on the south shore where you can enjoy an intimate dinner and dance on the patio next to the pool. Warm and friendly. (292–1935)

Paget Parish

Elbow Beach Hotel. Something is happening here every night of the week. Two seatings for dinner in the main *Terrace Room,* local entertainment in the nightclub and in the *Seahorse Pub,* weekly barbecues on the terrace, and Sunday brunch from 11:30 A.M. to 2 P.M. Casual dining with local specialties in the newly expanded *Seahorse Grill.* (295–3535)

Glencoe. Owners Reggie and Margot Cooper are justifiably proud of their chef, Roberta Williams, a graduate of the Culinary Institute of America and the only female head chef on the island. Ms. Williams turns out European-influenced dishes, as well as Bermudian specials (using fresh fish and produce). Lunches are served on the outside patio, and dinners in this magnificent manor house that dates from the early 1700s. (236–5274)

Harmony Club. French and Bermudian cuisine in pleasant, small restaurant; entertainment and dancing. (292–3500)

Horizons. Lovely dining room in an old hilltop Bermuda mansion; local entertainment and dancing. (295–0048)

Inverurie. *Great Sound House* restaurant overlooking the harbor. Dancing on the *Marine Terrace* and two shows nightly in *Le Cabaret.* (292–1000)

Newstead. Charming dining room in old Bermuda mansion full of antiques. Very Bermudian atmosphere and hospitality in this small hotel overlooking Hamilton and the harbor. Continental food and service, plus dancing. (292–6060)

Stonington Beach Hotel. Your chefs, wine stewards, waiters, hostess, pastry chef, dishwasher—all are eager students well on their way to graduation at the Stonington Beach Hotel, a hotel/school facility. Dinner is from 7 P.M. to 8:45 P.M. every evening. Each night is special: Musicians perform classical music every Monday; Wednesday is devoted to the cuisine of France; and on the last Thursday and Friday of each month, there is a ten-course gourmet dinner (prix fixe including service charge). Moderate. (236–5416)

Warwick Parish

Belmont Hotel. Lots of action here in the evening. Dinner and dancing in the *Terrace Cafe,* as well as shows four times weekly (Monday, Thursday, Friday, Saturday), local entertainment in the *Harbour Lounge* twice weekly (Tuesday and Saturday), and outdoor barbecues on the terrace overlooking the Great Sound. (295–1301)

Flamingo Beach Club. Relaxed dining here in a small property overlooking the south shore and private beach. Visitors welcome to friendly Bermudian atmosphere. (292–3761)

Mermaid Beach. The *Old Ship Pub* has nightly entertainment in this small charming hotel right on the water's edge. (295–5031)

Southampton Parish

The Greenhouse, Sonesta Beach Hotel. Lunch or dine inside the greathouse or on its wraparound terrace. The menu is consistently good: steaks (sirloin, tournedos, or steak Diana), veal (Oscar or Morels), fish (wahoo, salmon, Dover sole, or island-caught Bermuda). Expensive. (238–8122)

Pompano Beach Club. This small hotel has a dramatic location on a cliff above the ocean. Superb view from dining room and friendly atmosphere. (234–0222)

The Reefs. One of the nicest of the small hotels, tucked around its own cove on the south shore. From mid-May to Thanksgiving, lunch and dinner are served at *Coconuts,* a thatched-roof patio restaurant perched on a beachside cliff. Here, Austrian chef Herbie Gerzer turns out kebabs, steaks, fresh fish, and salads for lunch and more elaborate dishes at night. Gerzer is also responsible for the year-round formal presentations in the main house, and the new, adjacent, smoke-free, flower-filled conservatory. (238–0222)

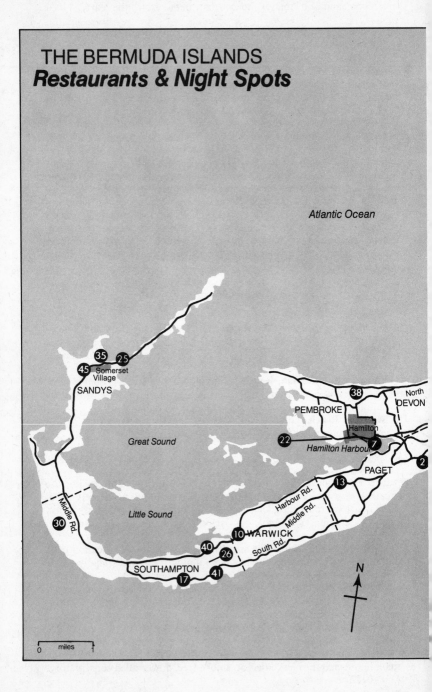

THE BERMUDA ISLANDS
Restaurants & Night Spots

Atlantic Ocean

35 25

45 Somerset
    Village

SANDYS

38

North
DEVON

PEMBROKE

Hamilton

Great Sound

22

Hamilton Harbour

7

PAGET

2

13

Harbour Rd.

Little Sound

Middle Rd.

Middle Rd.

30

10 WARWICK

40

26   South Rd.

SOUTHAMPTON

17   41

N

0   miles   1

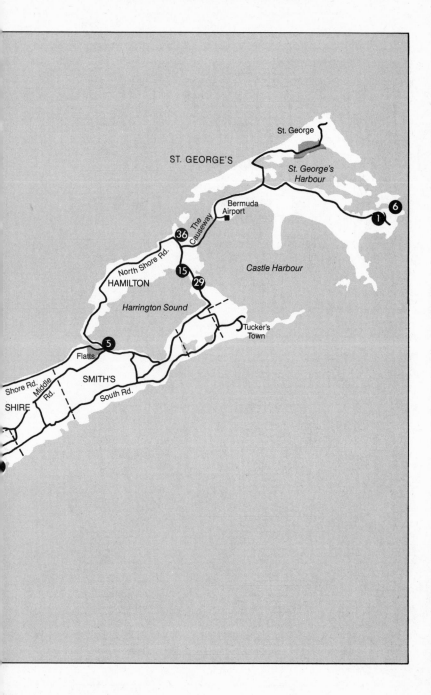

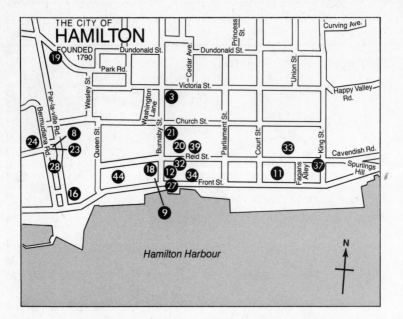

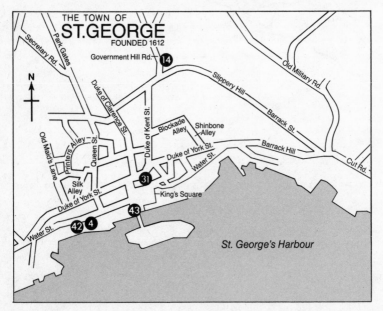

RESTAURANTS AND NIGHT SPOTS

1) Black Horse Tavern
2) Tavern on the Green
3) Romanoff*
4) Carriage House Restaurant
5) Inlet
6) Dennis Hideaway
7) Primavera
8) The Club*
9) Fisherman's Reef*
10) Flavors
11) Forty Thieves Club/Gombey Bar*
12) Conch Shell*
13) Fourways Inn
14) Gunpowder Cavern*
15) Tom Moore's Tavern
16) New Harbourfront*
17) Henry VIII Pub-Restaurant
18) Hog Penny Pub*
19) M.R. Onions*
20) Prego*
21) La Trattoria*
22) Harley's
23) Little Venice*
24) Lobster Pot*

25) Loyalty Inn
26) Newport Room
27) Oasis Club*
28) Portofino*
29) The Plantation
30) Port Royal Golf Club
31) Pub on the Square*
32) Loquats*
33) Bombay Bicycle Club*
34) Rum Runners*
35) Somerset Country Squire
36) Swizzle Inn
37) Show Bizz*
38) Once Upon a Table
39) Tivoli/Red Carpet*
40) Waterlot Inn
41) Whaler Inn
42) Wharf Tavern
43) White Horse Tavern*
44) Botanic Garden Tea Room*
45) Il Palio

*Number refers to detail maps

Southampton Princess. What isn't there here! Stop in the *Neptune Bar,* have a gourmet dinner in the *Newport Room* or regular hotel *(MAP)* dinner in *Windows on the Sound,* then move on to the *Empire Room,* where the most sophisticated entertainment on the island is featured. Or if you prefer a more casual evening, spend it in *Wickets.* Try also the *Rib Room/No. 1 Club* for lunch and dinner à la carte. Or if you prefer the romance of surfside dining and candlelight, take the jitney down to the *Whaler Inn* for dancing on the terrace. (238–8000)

Sandys Parish

Cambridge Beaches. This is the original cottage colony on the island and has maintained its high reputation for 50 years. Dining is gracious and elegant and there are barbecues, dancing, and entertainment on the terrace overlooking Mangrove Bay. Dance on millstones recovered from a British ship that went down on the reefs about 1818. A perfect place for romance! (234–0331)

Lantana Colony Club, Somerset Bridge. This club is currently one of Bermuda's "in" spots for social gatherings, making a reservation mandatory. (Dining hours are 7:30 to 9:30 nightly.) The menu at this award-winning restaurant is constantly changing, but the accent remains Continental and the ambience is definitely elegant. Entrees vary: fresh Bermuda tuna in a white wine sauce; roast duck in port wine sauce; filet of beef in a Rossini sauce; Bermuda lobster in season. The setting for dinner is in a distinctive main room with an adjacent solarium. Artwork hangs throughout, and service is formal. Expensive. (234–0141)

NIGHT SPOTS

Bermuda nightlife ranges from sophisticated clubs and discos to a few that are considered too wild for most visitors, but in comparison to New York or Paris, they may seem rather tame.

Some lively local clubs offer Bermuda entertainment from around 9 P.M. until the early A.M., and there are occasional imported acts at a few of the larger hotels. An increasing number of night spots are licensed to stay open until 3 A.M., and serve liquor to those over 18 years of age, with proof. Whether 18 or 80, expect a cover charge that hovers around $8 to $10 per person.

Clay House Inn, North Shore Road, Devonshire. Bermuda's oldest nightclub, about a 10-minute drive from Hamilton, this grande-dame is dedicated to entertaining visitors with "typical" all-Bermudian entertainment (that does include known names). The show starts nightly at 9:30 P.M. and goes to midnight, with a $10 per person cover charge that includes a complimentary drink. If you haven't stopped in yet, you should—it's a tradition. (292–3193)

The Club, on Bermudiana Road (above the *Little Venice* restaurant), Hamilton. This is another "in" place for upscale professionals. The club has a "brass and glass" look, with a small disco floor. A local D.J. mixes music to match dancers' moods, and may play calypso or reggae and then switch to the latest from London. The Club can hold about 150 guests at a time (each paying an $8 admission charge), and is open 7 nights a week, from 10 P.M. to 3 A.M. (295–6693)

Forty Thieves and Gombey Bar, Front Street, Hamilton. One of Bermuda's hot spots, with disco dancing every night, and shows scheduled throughout the season. Admission is $5 for dancing; $12 on show nights, which range from comedy reviews and jazz and rock groups to steel bands and island-hot calypso. (292–4040)

Oasis, Emporium Building, Front Street, Hamilton. Chic and trendy guests enter the second-story nightclub via a glass elevator with flashing lights. The main room of the disco is designed in salmon and mauve velveteen cushions set up in conversational groupings (a misnomer if ever there was one). The music that the local D.J. plays is loud and hot. The "greeter" at the entrance politely insures not only that everyone pays, but that men wear jackets and women are covered, if casual. An adjacent "Bambu Lounge" seats about 75, and is open in-season weekends, with live jazz setting a subtler pace. (292–4978)

Flavors, on Riddell's Bay (about five minutes from many south shore hotels), is as close to sophisticated sleaze as Bermuda permits, which makes it a very special spot. Open 7 nights a week throughout the year, with flashing disco lights and hot music that moves to an even hotter tempo. This is one of the few places where guests are permitted to wear jeans. (238–1987 or 238–1498)

The Swizzle Inn, on Middle Road, is about a half-mile from the airport. This pub is definitely for the younger crowd. The local hot-spot took its name from a bastardized roulette wheel that spins nightly from 4:30 P.M. to 6:30 P.M. with prices on it instead of numbers. Where it stops (at $1.50 to $2.00) is the price of rum drinks for the next half-hour, and then it spins again. Outside, it's Mopeds and motorcycle boots. Inside, a juke box plays hard and soft rock while players make bravado attempts at a dart board. Business cards from the four corners of the globe are tacked on ceiling, walls, and doors—yes, there is a *Fodor's Travel Guides* card there—we dare you to find it! (293–1854)

HOTEL NIGHT SPOTS

Belmont, Warwick Parish. Local entertainment nightly in the *Terrace Cafe* or *Harbour Lounge* (except Sunday) at 10:15 P.M. (295–1301)

Marriott's Castle Harbour Resort, Tucker's Town. Local entertainment and variety shows nightly throughout the property. Dancing until 1 A.M. (295–1211)

Elbow Beach, Paget. Local entertainment nightly except Friday. Showtime at 10 P.M. and dancing until 1 A.M. in *Peacock Room. Seahorse Pub* has its own, somewhat ribald, revue. (293–8161)

Grotto Bay, Hamilton Parish. Local entertainment nightly in clubhouse at 10:45 P.M. *Prospero's Cave* is a disco open from 9 P.M. to 1 A.M. (293–8333)

The Princess, Hamilton. Romantic dancing nightly in *Gazebo Lounge* overlooking Hamilton Harbour. Live band and recently expanded seating. (295–3000)

Sonesta Beach, Southampton Parish. A complete refurbishing and "face-lift" have made this standard a place to see and be seen. The posh supper club *Lillians* is a definite must, as are the other swinging special rooms inside the hotel. (238–8122)

Southampton Princess, Southampton. *The Empire Room* presents top international stars and local shows nightly. Show times are 10:15 P.M.

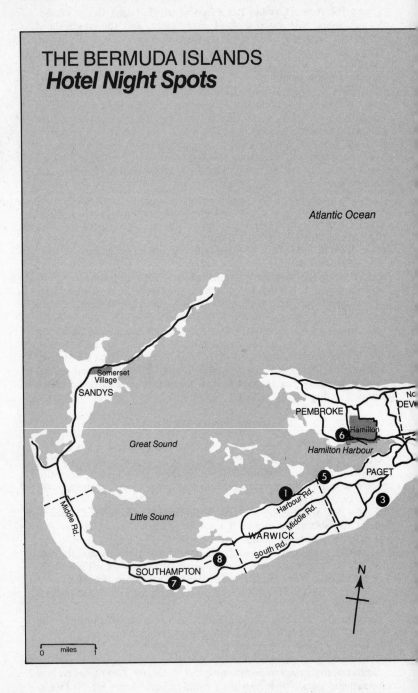

THE BERMUDA ISLANDS
Hotel Night Spots

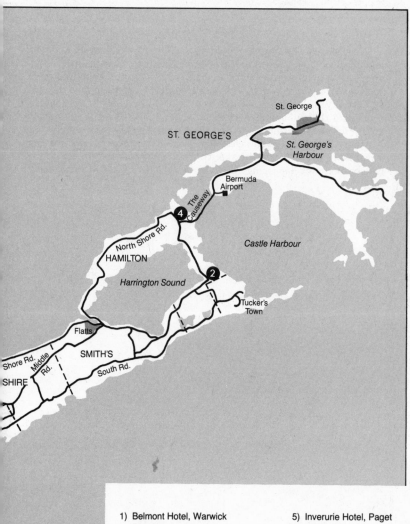

1) Belmont Hotel, Warwick
   Parish
2) Marriott's Castle Harbour,
   Tucker's Town
3) Elbow Beach Hotel,
   Paget Parish
4) Grotto Bay Hotel,
   Hamilton Parish
5) Inverurie Hotel, Paget
   Parish
6) Princess Hotel, City
   of Hamilton
7) Sonesta Beach Hotel,
   Southampton Parish
8) Southampton Princess
   Hotel, Southampton
   Parish

(local show) and 11:15 P.M. (international). *The Touch Club Discotheque* is open until 3 A.M. (238–8000)

FILMS, THEATER

Several hotels now have nightly in-house films for their guests, and two movie houses have opened in the heart of Hamilton. Local concerts and dramatic and ballet productions are held frequently throughout the year, and the *Bermuda Festival of Performing Arts* from mid-January to the end of February each year draws top international artists of theater, dance, opera, and classical and modern music. Check "This Week in Bermuda" and "Preview of Bermuda" to find the weekly calendar of events.

Almost all hotels and cottage colonies have *The Royal Gazette,* the national newspaper, on your breakfast tray. It's the best way to get up-to-date on Bermuda happenings. True Bermuda buffs receive overseas mailings.

INDEX

Index

Practical Information

(See second index for place names, sights, and special events listings)

Fodor's Travel Guides

U.S. Guides

Alaska
Arizona
Atlantic City & the
  New Jersey Shore
Boston
California
Cape Cod
Carolinas & the
  Georgia Coast
The Chesapeake Region
Chicago
Colorado
Dallas & Fort
  Worth

Disney World & the
  Orlando Area
Florida
Hawaii
Houston &
  Galveston
Las Vegas
Los Angeles, Orange
  County, Palm Springs
Maui
Miami, Fort Lauderdale,
  Palm Beach
Michigan, Wisconsin,
  Minnesota

New England
New Mexico
New Orleans
New Orleans (Pocket
  Guide)
New York City
New York City (Pocket
  Guide)
New York State
Pacific North Coast
Philadelphia
The Rockies
San Diego
San Francisco

San Francisco (Pocket
  Guide)
The South
Texas
USA
Virgin Islands
Virginia
Waikiki
Washington, DC
Williamsburg

Foreign Guides

Acapulco
Amsterdam
Australia, New Zealand,
  The South Pacific
Austria
Bahamas
Bahamas (Pocket
  Guide)
Baja & the Pacific
  Coast Resorts
Barbados
Belgium & Luxembourg
Bermuda
Brazil
Britain (Great Travel
  Values)
Budget Europe
Canada
Canada (Great Travel
  Values)
Canada's Atlantic
  Provinces
Cancún, Cozumel,
  Mérida, the
  Yucatán
Caribbean

Caribbean (Great
  Travel Values)
Central America
China
China's Great Cities
Eastern Europe
Egypt
Europe
Europe's Great Cities
Florence & Venice
France
France (Great Travel
  Values)
Germany
Germany (Great Travel
  Values)
Great Britain
Greece
The Himalayan
  Countries
Holland
Hong Kong
Hungary
India, including Nepal
Ireland
Israel

Italy
Italy (Great Travel
  Values)
Jamaica
Japan
Japan (Great Travel
  Values)
Jordan & the Holy Land
Kenya, Tanzania,
  the Seychelles
Korea
Lisbon
Loire Valley
London
London (Great Travel
  Values)
London (Pocket Guide)
Madrid & Barcelona
Mexico
Mexico City
Montreal &
  Quebec City
Munich
New Zealand
North Africa
Paris

Paris (Pocket Guide)
Portugal
Rio de Janeiro
The Riviera (Fun on)
Rome
Saint Martin &
  Sint Maarten
Scandinavia
Scandinavian Cities
Scotland
Singapore
South America
South Pacific
Southeast Asia
Soviet Union
Spain
Spain (Great Travel
  Values)
Sweden
Switzerland
Sydney
Tokyo
Toronto
Turkey
Vienna
Yugoslavia

Special-Interest Guides

Bed & Breakfast
  Guide: North America
Health & Fitness
  Vacations

Royalty Watching
Selected Hotels of
  Europe

Selected Resorts
  and Hotels of the U.S.
Shopping in Europe

Skiing in North
  America
Sunday in New York